Good
choices

A Lucky Duck Book

Good Choices

Teaching young people aged 8 to 11 to make positive decisions about their own lives

Tina Rae

P·C·P

Paul Chapman
Publishing

Paul Chapman Publishing
A SAGE Publications Company
1 Oliver's Yard
55 City Road
London EC1Y 1SP

SAGE Publications Inc.
2455 Teller Road
Thousand Oaks, California 91320

SAGE Publications India Pvt Ltd.
B-42, Panchsheel Enclave
Post Box 4109
New Delhi 110 017

Commissioning Editors: Barbara Maines and George Robinson
Editorial Team: Mel Maines, Sarah Lynch, Wendy Ogden
Designer: Nick Shearn
Illustrator: Mark Ruffle

A catalogue record for this book is available from the British Library

Library of Congress Control Number 2005907008

ISBN10 1-4129-1818-9
ISBN13 978-1-4129-1818-3
ISBN10 1-4129-1819-7 (pbk)
ISBN13 1-4129-1819-0 (pbk)

Printed on paper from sustainable resources.

Printed in Great Britain by The Cromwell Press Ltd, Trowbridge, Wiltshire.

Contents

How to use the CD-ROM

The CD-ROM contains PDF files, labelled 'Colour illustrations.pdf' and 'Line illustrations.pdf' which consist of posters and drawings to colour in for each lesson in this resource. You will need Acrobat Reader version 3 or higher to view and print these resources.

The documents are set up to print to A4 but you can enlarge them to A3 by increasing the output percentage at the point of printing using the page set-up settings for your printer.

Preface

Making choices is central to the human condition. From the moment we become conscious human beings we can begin to choose how we respond and with whom we interact in the social world. The ability to choose increases through time. The individual's self-awareness, self-esteem, locus of control (that is, the ability to gain internal control) all impact upon these choices and the ways in which they are made.

The stories in this series are based around the problems and joys of living as a child and young person within the twenty first century. They highlight the essential choices that people have to make in order to survive and function in a world that can seem complex and, at times, difficult to understand.

This series consists of three books which aim to help children and young people to make the kinds of choices that will achieve the best possible outcomes. There is consequently a focus throughout on the ways in which both feelings and the brain inform behaviour and our capacity to influence and make good life choices. The intention is to encourage the listener to become aware of the differences between thinking, feeling and behaving and the ways in which they can distinguish between responses based on thoughts or feelings and the majority of responses which are based on both. The aim is to encourage them to distinguish between impulsive or well thought out responses which allow for good and positive outcomes.

The series provides a 'safe' medium, the story, in which children can both identify and reflect upon good and negative choices and the outcomes that will ensue from both. Each book is designed to target a specific age range from early years to late adolescence. There are themes that are common to all three books. These include issues such as bullying, racism, inclusion, peer pressure, grief, loss, separation and coping with change among others which are pertinent to young people's lives and experiences.

Each book contains a series of stories which include opportunities for discussion, reflection and a range of follow on and reinforcement activities. There is a focus throughout on creativity and problem-solving which can be undertaken within a climate of empathy, tolerance and mutual support. The stories in the series would fulfil many of the PSHE/Citizenship requirements. Although the primary aim of the stories is to help children to make good choices and to become good citizens, we would emphasise the importance of the stories themselves. They are not merely didactic tools. They are meant to be read or listened to and enjoyed in their own right.

Margaret Collins, Tina Rae and Phil Carradice

Introduction and Background

Traditional behaviourist views of behaviour see it as being a function of the environment whilst cognitive views of behaviour deem it to be a product of personal variables (Kendall 1993). These contrast to the Cognitive Behavioural model which views personal variables, that is, thoughts and feelings and the environment as forming a 'mutual influence system'. As Kendall states:

> 'Cognitive Behavioural Therapy focuses on how people respond to their cognitive interpretations of experiences rather than the environment or the experience itself and how thoughts and behaviours are related. It combines cognition change procedures with behavioural contingency management and learning experiences designed to change distorted or deficient information processing.'

This approach is basically based on the premise that personal 'problems' tend to occur due to irrational thinking and that the main cause of so called unwanted behaviour is the connection between thoughts and emotions (Ronen 1997).

As Gourley (1999) states:

> A blend of cognitive and behavioural techniques are used to firstly raise awareness of the self and one's emotions, and secondly to modify thought processes through a variety of strategies, including altering perceptions, attributions and expectations, initiating internal dialogue through positive self-talk and self-instruction; using self-monitoring and self-reward; and developing problem-solving skills. These techniques require the individual's active participation in changing thinking and altering behaviour. (p9)

Cognitive and affective domains

Being aware that both feelings and the brain inform our behaviours is crucial if we are to develop the capacity for making good choices. As stated earlier, it is possible to modify thought processes and develop problem-solving skills through a variety of strategies. However, in this series, we are not specifically aiming to introduce such strategies and present them to students as their range of options. Rather, the intention here is to encourage students to become aware of the differences between thinking, feeling and behaviour and the ways in which they can use both the brain and feelings in order to inform behaviour. They can and should be able to distinguish between responses which are based upon thoughts or feelings and the majority of our responses which are based upon both. This will also then, in turn, allow them to distinguish between impulsive and well thought out reactions and behaviours, consequently allowing for good choices which will gain them the best possible outcomes.

This programme provides students with opportunities to further understand these distinctions within a safe medium, that is, the story, in which they have the opportunity to both identify and reflect upon good choices and outcomes that they may or may not make.

Locus of control

Key to this process is the concept of locus of control. The stories in the programme show children reacting to certain contexts and situations and having both internal and external control – internal control being or feeling that you are in control or responsible for your own behaviours and responses and external control feeling that you are being controlled or that your behaviours are the direct result of others behaviour and responses or the context in which you find yourself. There is a strong emphasis on the need to develop internal control in order to make good choices and to develop and sustain positive behaviour. Acceptance of the consequences of behaviours and the importance of understanding how our feelings and thoughts impact upon them are also key.

Emotional literacy and mental health

Consequently, many of the stories in this programme show characters dealing with a range of problems and dilemmas in which they have to make choices about the ways in which they respond. These choices are frequently dependent upon their ability to successfully engage with both the brain and feelings in order to inform behaviour and the way in which they are able to effectively cope with and manage their feelings. The latter concept of emotional literacy is also central to this programme. There is, throughout each story, a focus on encouraging students to reflect upon their feelings and behaviours and to also successfully recognise, label and cope with the range of feelings that they will experience on a daily basis. There is a great deal of research which links children's mental health and physical health to the development of emotional literacy (Goleman 1995, Grant 1992, Rudd 1998). Peter Sharp (2001) suggests four main reasons why emotional literacy must be promoted in both children and adults. He states that we need to:

1. recognise our emotions in order to be able to label and define them

2. understand our emotions in order to become effective learners

3. handle and manage our emotions in order to be able to develop and sustain positive relationships

4. appropriately express emotions in order to develop as rounded people who are able to help ourselves and, in turn, those around us.

The latter reason also implies that in order to help ourselves and consequently make good choices which allow us to change, adapt and successfully operate within the social context, we need to develop internal control alongside the ability to positively utilise both brain and feelings to inform our behaviours. This includes recognising and preventing impulsive responses when they are not helpful and also the ability to think, that is, use the brain to identify consequences, looking ahead in order to identify consequences and make a good choice which will achieve the best possible outcome.

As Rae, Marris and Koeries (2005) state:

> Building emotional literacy and providing children with daily opportunities to develop their skills in this area will also simultaneously help to promote good mental health and nurture children's ability to be resilient and to cope with the challenges that life may bring them. (p.27)

Challenges and pressures

Coping with such challenges and pressures is, of course, a reality of everyday life for children and students. It is therefore essential that they develop the emotional resilience and ability to engage the brain and feelings to inform behaviours and make choices that will ensure positive outcomes. The challenges and pressures are many and varied but for the purpose of this programme the following have been highlighted:

▶ coping with injustice
▶ coping with racism
▶ coping with labelling
▶ taking care of the environment
▶ bullying
▶ peer pressure
▶ breaking rules
▶ grief, loss and separation
▶ telling the truth
▶ coping with change.

Within all these varying areas, students will be required to make choices about the way in which they respond and behave. It is hoped that this programme will provide them with the opportunities to develop the skills and self-awareness needed to make good life choices which are positive for themselves and those with whom they live and work.

Aims of the programme

This programme has been developed in order to help students develop the ability to make good choices and to make use of both brain and feelings to inform behaviours which will achieve them the best possible outcomes. The aims of the programme are as follows:

▶ to enable students to understand how thoughts, feelings and behaviours are related

▶ to encourage students to develop self-control and internal control

▶ to enable students to develop self-talk (Michenbaum 1977) and self-reflection strategies in order to modify and inform behaviours

▶ for students to be able to recognise impulsive responses and learn to use the brain in order to inhibit these

▶ to develop empathy and more awareness of other's intentions

▶ to understand and identify a connection between behaviour and other's responses to these behaviours

▶ for students to be able to more accurately predict their own behaviours and to identify the consequences of their behaviours

▶ to encourage students to identify solutions and good choices via small steps as opposed to simply emphasising ends or goals

▶ to encourage students to generate a range of alternative solutions

▶ to enable students to identify the feelings that they experience and to gain a deeper understanding of them

▶ to further develop self-knowledge, self-esteem and self-worth

▶ for students to affirm the validity of others positions and feelings and to respect and accept differences in order to promote a sense of equality

▶ to encourage students to develop problem-solving skills within a supportive group context, recognising how they can learn from each other's experience

▶ to encourage students to identify problems as challenges which can be met by their own resources, skills and support systems.

The extent to which these objectives are met is perhaps the best indicator as to the success of the programme as a whole.

Structure of the Sessions

Each of the sessions is structured as follows:

Focus and summary

The main focus points are highlighted prior to a brief summary of the ensuing story. These can be used simply to inform the facilitator or as part of an introduction for the students in the group. The facilitator may wish to record the focus points on a whiteboard or flip-chart prior to the start of the session and to use the summary script as a prompt.

The story and Flag points

The facilitator reads the story to the students. Flag points are indicated within the text in order to pick up on key themes or raise particular points of interest with the students. The facilitator can choose to stop at each point or to read the story straight through, stopping at the end in order to use these as discussion points prior to completing the activities. The questions are not intended as any kind of straitjacket and it is presumed that the facilitator will tailor these to the needs of the target group.

Each story is provided with two endings, both of which can be read to the students. The facilitator can then ask them to discuss these endings and to identify which would achieve the best possible outcome for the characters involved. A particular focus here is on identifying the choices made and whether or not these were the best or most informed choices, that is, incorporating both brain and feelings to inform behaviour.

Activities

A range of follow-on or reinforcement activities are then provided in order to further clarify or build on key concepts or themes encountered in the story. The first activity takes the form of a Circle Time problem-solving activity in which students are required to consider the two endings prior to formulating what they perceive to be the best possible ending or outcome – what would have been the best choice and why? This activity is followed by two or three further tasks which may be undertaken on the basis of interest or available time. It is not intended that all activities should be completed in one session and it would seem appropriate for the facilitator and students to select on the basis of group interest.

Work outside school

This activity is intended to be undertaken outside of the school context and will usually require students to involve others in gathering information and investigating views and available resources.

Reflection

The final reflection points are intended to aid students in the process of personal reflection. As with the activities, it may not be possible to cover all the questions and ideas within the session. The facilitator may wish to record the reflection points or questions within an A4 'take home' sheet for students to work through in their own time. Alternatively, reflection time may be allocated in addition to this session. What is important is to stress how stopping to think and reflect upon our feelings, thoughts and behaviours can aid us in the process of making good choices.

Setting up the programme

The sessions in this programme are set out in a structured way but this format is not intended to be inflexible. Some facilitators may wish to adapt the resources as they go along, in tune with the responses and interests of the individual students. The story and reflection approach certainly allows for such flexibility and encourages students to pursue ideas and themes of particular interest at any point in the session. However, for convenience and ease of use the framework provided does seem to be useful and facilitate the central objectives. It may be helpful for the facilitator to take note of the following points when setting up the activities.

Size of group

This programme is designed to be delivered to whole classes but can also easily be adapted for smaller groups of students. However the teaching group is arranged, it is important to ensure that all students have the facility to participate and reflect within the session. Adequate talk time is essential if students are really to benefit from the course content and begin to develop their skills.

Setting the tone

It is essential to set the tone for these sessions right at the start of the programme and to particularly emphasise the way in which all views and contributions are to be listened to and valued. As a key aim of the programme is to help students to understand and make good choices, it is vital that the climate of the group is both supportive and nurturing from the outset.

It is consequently suggested that discussions are conducted initially via the Circle Time process. Group rules will need to be agreed at the outset and subsequently adhered to by all involved.

Using the stories and activities

The stories are designed to facilitate students' problem-solving skills and skills of self-reflection and self-awareness. The Flag points are intended to pick out key themes and ideas and to prompt the above processes. It is consequently vital to ensure adequate discussion time as suggested earlier. It is entirely at the facilitator's discretion as to how these questions are covered. For some, it may seem more comfortable and logical to stop at each marked stage in the story whilst for others it may be more practical to read the story without stopping and then pose the questions altogether. This may be to some extent dependent upon the age, concentration and memory levels of the individuals being targeted.

It is important to emphasise that none of the endings are the right endings. There are advantages and disadvantages in all of them and the most important thing is for students to be able to analyse the choices, decisions and actions taken by the individual characters in the stories. Once again, allocating adequate time for this purpose is essential as is ensuring an open forum for debate via the Circle Time process.

It is recommended that the latter is used to facilitate the initial problem-solving activity in each session and that the facilitator is aware of and confident in making use of this framework. It is not anticipated that all the activities are undertaken in one session. It is entirely up to the facilitator and students as to which activities are deemed to be most appropriate. It may be the case that an entirely different activity is developed as a result of the story and question process. Ultimately, this is a flexible framework and it is not anticipated that the scheme is strictly adhered to. It is more important that the students' interests and ideas are given space for development.

It will also be important to approach work outside school with sensitivity. Parents or carers will need to understand the nature of the programme and the ways in which it aims to aid students develop problem-solving skills and self-reflection skills in order to identify and make good choices. It may be helpful to provide a brief outline of the course and its key objectives with a brief description of the approaches adopted and the way that students are being encouraged to utilise both brain and feelings in order to inform the decision-making process.

Forward thinking

It is hoped that this programme will be an enjoyable learning experience for both the students and staff involved and that the linkage made between the affective and cognitive domains will continue to positively inform future choices and decision-making. For this to happen, it is suggested that staff should consider how making emotionally literate choices can be included both through and beyond the taught curriculum. This programme needs to be viewed as a prompt to this wider process of providing all students with both the forum and the skills needed to make good life choices – ones which ensure both the mental well-being and safety of both themselves and those in their communities and social contexts.

Bibliography

Goleman, D. (1995) *Emotional Intelligence, Why it Matters More than IQ*, London, Bloomsbury.

Gourley, P. (1999) *Teaching Self-control in the Classroom, A Cognitive Behavioural Approach*, Bristol, Lucky Duck Publishing.

Grant, W.T. (1992) *Consortium on the School Based Promotion of Social Competence, Drugs and Alcohol Prevention Curricula*, San Francisco, Josey-Bass.

Johnson, P. & Rae, T. (1999) *Crucial Skills – An Anger Management and Problem-solving Teaching Programme for High School Students*, Bristol, Lucky Duck Publishing.

Kendall, P.C. (1993) *Cognitive – Behavioural Therapies with Youth: Guiding Theory. Current Status and Emerging Development. Journal of Consulting and Clinical Psychology* 61(2) 2 35-247.

Koeries, J., Marris, B. & Rae, T. (2005) *Problem Postcards, Social, Emotional and Behavioural Skills Training for Disaffected and Difficult Children aged 7 to 11*, Bristol, Lucky Duck Publishing.

Rae, T. (1998) *Dealing with Feeling*, Bristol, Lucky Duck Publishing.

Rae, T. (2001) *Strictly Stress – Effective Stress Management for High School Students*, Bristol, Lucky Duck Publishing.

Ronen, T. (1997) *Cognitive Developmental Therapy with Young Children*, Wiley, England.

Rudd, B. (1998) *Talking is for Kids*, Bristol, Lucky Duck Publishing

Sharp, P. (2001) *Nurturing Emotional Literacy: A Practical Guide for Teachers, Parents and those in the Caring Professions*, London, David Fulton Publishers.

Wardle, C. & Rae, T. (2002) *School Survival – Helping Students Survive and Achieve in Secondary School*, Bristol, Lucky Duck Publishing.

The Stories and Activities

Session I: Caught in the Act

 Focus

▸ distinguishing between right and wrong

▸ thinking ahead to the consequences

▸ dealing with peer pressure

▸ using the brain and feelings to inform behaviour

▸ recognising and empathising with the feelings of others.

This story is about a group of children who develop a system of successfully stealing from their local corner shop. There is a considerable amount of peer pressure from some members of the group to conform to this pattern of behaviour. It is only when one member of the group is 'caught in the act' that they are made fully aware of the consequences of their behaviour, that is, the fact that stealing is not such a good choice.

Either stop the story and discuss the Flag points as you read or read the whole story and use these as discussion points prior to completing the activities.

Jason and Alec had been best friends since they first started at Netherwood Primary. They were like two peas in a pod according to their mums. Not only did they look identical, but they also loved the same foods, computer games and playing out and they'd both recently been picked for their local football team. This was generally considered to be a great honour and had certainly raised their profile in their new high school. This was really important as anyone who has gone from Year 6 to Year 7 knows. It is a really big change and not easy to suddenly go from being top dog to the bottom of the heap again. As Jason said, 'It's like you've got to prove yourself all over again so that you don't get pushed around by the other kids.'

 Flag: How do you think you would feel (did feel) when making this transition from primary to secondary school? Do you think this would be a difficult time for most students? What sort of help and support do you think people would need in order to feel safe and secure?

13

Alec liked hanging around with Jason – mainly because he seemed to find it so much easier to make friends and didn't seem to get shy or nervous when he met new people. Although everyone else seemed to think of them as being very similar, Alec didn't really agree. He felt that Jason was far more confident than he was. The fact that he'd formed his own gang since he'd arrived at Netherwood High only seemed to prove this fact still further. Still, Alex wasn't complaining. It was just good to have some more mates to hang around with and they all seemed to like having a laugh. Joe, Cara and Rocky all seemed to enjoy doing wild things. They were always messing about in lessons but they seemed to know when to cool it so they didn't get into any big trouble.

Flag: What do you think it is that makes someone feel more confident? What kinds of things can help people to feel more confident? How do friends help us to feel better about ourselves? Is it a good thing to rely on others to make us feel positive? When is 'having a laugh' not such a positive thing?

Anyway, during the last two weeks they had developed a new game. It wasn't one for school but something they had started to do on their way to and from school. Cara had been the first one to suggest it. She had been joking with Alec about the fact that his mum didn't like him eating too much chocolate or junk food. He was only allowed one packet of low calorie crisps in his lunch box every day and one cereal bar – no chocolate, no Pringles and definitely no white bread.

'She must be dead posh, your mum. I don't think mine even knows they make bread that isn't sliced.' She laughed out loud. Alec didn't mind too much. She was only teasing and he knew his mum was over the top about all her health stuff. She was never out of the gym herself and even wrote down everything that she ate each day. It drove his dad mad but Alec had just made his mind up to ignore it.

Flag: Do you think Cara knew that she wouldn't really hurt Alec's feelings? How would she be able to make this judgement? When do you think teasing others is OK? When wouldn't it be OK?

Anyway, after she'd finished joking around, Cara turned and looked directly at Alec.

'You know, it doesn't matter what you have and haven't got in your lunch. We can soon sort it out. In fact, we can get you whatever you want.'

'How's that?' asked Alec.

Jason laughed and winked at Cara. 'I'll tell you what we can do – just take what we want from Mr Hedges shop. He's such an old geezer, there's no way he'd ever notice. It's not like he's got eyes in the back of his head is it? Anyway, he makes loads of money. My dad's always said everything is overpriced in that shop – even double on some things you'd get in Tescos.'

Flag: What do you think of Cara's idea? How do you think Jason is feeling now? What do you think he is thinking? Is stealing from a shop wrong? Is there an occasion when stealing of this kind might be the right thing to do?

Alec smiled. He really liked his new friends. They just seemed to make everything more exciting and such a laugh. He smiled back at Cara and that's really how it all began. From then on, they'd take it in turns to steal from the shop. At first it was just small things like chewing gum or a packet of crisps but as they got more confident, they'd go for bigger items. Cara had managed to steal a whole set of hair accessories for her younger sister's birthday and the box measured at least 80cm square. How she managed to get it out of the shop without being spotted was a real miracle according to Rocky. But they were all good at keeping watch and took it in turns to go up to the counter in order to distract Mr Hedges. Sometimes that meant buying a small item from him and talking about his dog for five minutes but they all managed it.

Alec didn't mind chatting to Mr Hedges. He actually thought he was a nice old man as he always smiled and told them silly jokes. Alec opted to distract him on the majority of their visits to the shop and tended to let the others get on with the stealing. That was until Joe seemed to notice and started to say stuff about it to the rest of the gang. 'I don't think Alec's that good at lifting – maybe he needs a bit more practice,' he joked. Alec went red. He felt stupid and he knew he'd have to join in a bit more if he was going to remain a member of the gang.

Flag: How do you think Mr Hedges would feel if he knew what the gang were actually doing? Why did Alec think he'd have to join in more? What was he thinking and feeling when he came under pressure in this way? Why did he seem to 'automatically' conform?

So, the next day on the way home from school, he volunteered to steal five notebooks and pens, four packets of salt and vinegar crisps and four bottles of diet coke. He was wearing his over-sized fleece which had a total of six pockets so he knew he'd have enough room to hide it all. Cara had gone over to the counter to talk to Mr Hedges. At this point, Alec actually turned and stared directly at him. It was almost as if he was willing Mr. Hedges to notice that he was up to something and somehow try and stop him. He didn't know how or why, but that's how he felt.

Ending point: At this point, the following two endings can be read to the students. The facilitator can then ask the students to judge which is the better ending, that is, which one would achieve the best possible outcome for those involved. The students can then be asked to work out the best ending for themselves via the first Circle Time activity listed in the Activities section.

Ending one

Mr Hedges looked more closely at Alec and smiled. 'You know,' he said, 'You lot come in my shop every day. You never buy that much, but you're always so polite and take the time to chat to me. I appreciate that you know. There's not many kids that would bother.'

Alec went redder than ever. He didn't know where to look. Cara turned round and nudged him. She was obviously finding it hard to keep a straight face.

'That's a nice thing to say,' she said.

'Well, I think I'll give you all a treat for being such good customers. Why don't you all have a drink and some crisps on the house? It's not every day I feel like being so generous so just make the most of it.'

The gang all smiled and did as they were told. Cara giggled throughout the whole process. She obviously found it really funny but Alec just felt uncomfortable, mainly because he couldn't believe that he was still going to have to nick all the other stuff. Joe had made that clear as they all went over to get their crisps.

'Don't forget,' he said 'You've still got to get the rest of the stuff.'

Alec felt sick but he took a deep breath and started to fill his pockets. Then he felt a hand on his right shoulder. He looked around and saw Mr. Clark the Science teacher standing directly behind him. He looked absolutely furious.

'Helping yourself are you?' he said.

Alec was speechless. He just hung his head. When he looked up he saw that the others had all run out of the shop. It was just him.

Ending two

Mr Hedges was looking very strange. In fact, almost like he was ill or becoming ill. Alec walked over to him.

'Are you OK?' he asked.

'Yes, I think so. I just had a sort of pain in my chest – you know – nothing serious but I think I'll just take a seat behind the counter if you don't mind.' Alec helped him to move across to the side of the counter.

'Are you sure you're OK? I could phone for the ambulance if you're still dodgy,' he said.

'No, no – you're alright, no worries. I just need to catch my breath. That's better. Anyway, what do you want today?' Alec went red. He suddenly remembered. He looked round and saw Cara stuffing three packets of crisps into her bag. He quickly turned round, bought a packet of chewies and left the shop. The others were waiting outside. They were all laughing as Cara handed round the crisps.

'Well, I guess we'll just have to accept you as you are,' she laughed.

'Yeah,' said Joe, 'You'll never be that good at nicking so perhaps you'd better stick to being a decoy. Here, have a crisp.'

He handed the packet to Alec. Alec smiled lamely as he opened them. 'Well, it wasn't so bad after all,' he thought. 'At least I'm still in the gang and at least I still got my crisps.'

Activities

Use Circle Time as a vehicle to problem-solve. Ask the students to work out for themselves what would be a better ending to this story. What do they think should have happened and why? What do they think would have been the best choice for Alec?

The need to feel part of a group is very strong and sometimes feeling accepted can be more important to us than anything else. Ask students to discuss times when they may have felt like this. How did their feelings affect their behaviours? Did they stop to think ahead or merely act on the basis of feelings and how wise were the choices they then made?

Students can make lists of behaviours they consider to be 'right' and 'wrong' and then focus on the question, 'What would happen if we always did the 'wrong' thing?'

What kinds of rules do we need in order to ensure that both ourselves and others remain safe? The students can brainstorm a list of 'respectful rules'.

Work outside school

If someone was a victim of crime and had something stolen from them or had been mugged, what sort of help can they expect from within the community? The students can be asked to investigate this and to liaise with others such as the Police, Youth Offending Team and Neighbourhood Watch. They can report back and collate information into a display or information booklet.

Reflection

Ask the students to consider a time when they let their feelings 'rule their heads' and did not stop to reflect upon the consequences of their actions. What happened? Was the outcome positive or negative for them and for others involved? Do they think that the outcome would have been better if they had identified their feelings and how these might affect their behaviours before acting?

How do we make 'good choices'? Do we need to engage with our feelings and thoughts before acting?

Do we need to have a 'thinking heart' and a 'feeling brain' or a combination of both?

Session 2: The Lie

Focus

▸ distinguishing between truth and fiction in real life

▸ using brain and feelings to inform behaviour

▸ impulsive responses and their consequences

▸ thinking ahead to the consequences.

This story is about a group of children who try to avoid getting into trouble by lying their way out of it. There is an incident in the playground during one lunch break when three panes of glass are broken. The boy who kicked the ball instinctively lies when tackled by the member of staff on duty and the other children in the group feel that they have to then substantiate his story. The end result is that all the children lie in order to avoid the consequences of their actions. This leads to some uncomfortable feelings and moments and prompts the listener to focus on the difficulties surrounding impulsive lying and responses.

Either stop the story and discuss the Flag points as you read or read the whole story and use these as discussion points prior to completing the activities.

Kera, Stephen, Alban and Ellen were probably the best footballers in the whole school – well, certainly in Year 8. They had all had an absolute passion for football since primary school and this was evident in school and outside of school where all of them did nothing but seemingly eat, drink and sleep the game. Kera was determined to emulate the girls in *Bend it like Beckham*. She was desperate to go to the States once she had taken her GCSEs and play for one of their major league teams. It was odd that, just like in the film, her dad simply laughed at her when she told him. 'What on earth would they want to employ a scrawny little girl like you for?' he'd said, laughing. Kera didn't mind though – she knew that she was good, but she also knew that she had to continue to practice in order to really achieve her goals. There was no way that she could rest on her laurels for one moment. There was simply too much competition, including her best friends.

Flag: How do you think that Kera really felt about her dad's comments? Why does it seem to matter so much what parents and carers think of us and say about us? Do you think his attitude will eventually hinder or help Kera?

Anyway, the lunchtime in question was a really good opportunity for all of them to practise their skills. This was mainly because there were at least six members of staff off sick which meant that there was very little supervision. Everyone loved it when that happened. It meant you could really go wild and do whatever you wanted. Of course, you couldn't do anything illegal. There were still enough people hanging around to see if you crept behind the bike sheds for a cigarette but you could manage to get extended periods on the football pitch without anyone noticing. Stephen was particularly pleased as he had had no time to train during the last two days and they had a big match coming up at the weekend. He knew he needed to get to optimum fitness if he was going to manage to save as many goals as he did last month. They had made him 'Man of the Match' then but he knew he had been slipping since then. He was starting to feel quite irritated and nervous and all the others had noticed how twitchy he had become.

'He keeps snapping at me all the time,' said Ellen. 'It's really starting to get on my nerves.'

'I know,' said Kera, 'But don't get at him as well. The last thing we all need is a big argument. We need to keep calm if we are going to be able to do our best on Saturday.'

Flag: Why do you think that people take out their anger and stress on those who are closest to them? Do you think Stephen was right to snap at his friends? What do you think he could have done in order to cope better with his feelings? What do you think would happen to his relationships if he continued to act in an aggressive way towards his friends?

As they ran out on to the pitch, Ellen could see that Stephen's face was quite pink. She was glad that he was going to run round the pitch for a bit. He needed to let some of that anger and energy out and she didn't want it directed at her again. They all decided to run ten laps prior to practising their passes. By the time they had run round the pitch six times, all of them were beginning to sweat and flag a little bit. Alban was the only one who seemed remotely confident that he could continue and manage all ten laps. He had only been training seriously for about twelve months and it irritated Stephen that he should have become so fit so easily. It always seemed to be such hard work for him to maintain his level of fitness.

'It's just not fair,' he thought as he watched Alban sprint ahead of them on the sixth lap. What was even more irritating was the fact that Alban then turned round and grinned at them all as he raced ahead.

Ellen looked at Stephen and said, 'Don't worry, he's only teasing.' 'Yeah, but it's dead irritating,' said Stephen. 'He's such a plonker at times. He really gets on my nerves.' Ellen looked across and winked at Kera. They both seemed to know what to do next.

'Come on, Stephen. We know you're brilliant,' said Ellen. 'Just show us what you're made of.'

'Yeah, come on,' said Kera. 'We know you can beat us any day.' Stephen looked at them. He'd usually laugh at this point. The girls were quite good at cheering him up but his mood was too entrenched today. He just looked at them both.

'Huh,' he said, 'It is not exactly difficult to beat two skinny girls like you is it?' Ellen blushed. She hated being called skinny and Kera just turned away. She knew it just wasn't worth the confrontation.

Flag: How do you think Kera knew that it wasn't worth the confrontation? What do you think would have happened if she had tackled Stephen about his rudeness at this point? Is it always right to confront someone if they have upset you? When would you confront someone straight away and when would you wait a while? What does waiting enable us to do?

Stephen ran off and the girls followed him. By the time all of them had completed the final lap they were all pretty tired. However, Stephen insisted that they go out onto the pitch and practise their moves. They had about ten minutes left of the lunch break and all of them were keen to get as much practice in as possible. There was also plenty of room on the pitch. Most of the kids in their year group weren't at all bothered about playing football and regarded those who were interested as odd. All of them had had to put up with a considerable amount of abuse, frequently being shouted at as they ran out on to the pitch every lunch and break time. Most of the abuse centred on them wearing their kit in school. They frequently heard names such as, 'anorak', 'gay', 'poofter' and other such terms of abuse being screamed across the playground as they ran out onto the pitch. However, they didn't care. None of them minded being considered different and as Kera always said, 'There's strength in numbers you know.'

Flag: Do you think it's true that there is strength in numbers? Why do people seem to get irritated by others who seem to be different in some way? Do they feel threatened? Do you think they should feel threatened?

Five minutes after they had run out onto the pitch, the whistle went. Kera, Alban and Ellen all looked at Stephen who by now was absolutely purple in the face. It was evident that he was really angry. He picked up the ball and kicked it as hard as he possibly could into the school building. The others followed the ball until it reached the side of the gym. Kera held her breath. For some reason she seemed to know what was going to happen next. As they watched, the ball went straight through the wall-to-wall pane of glass, shattering it completely. Fortunately for the students standing outside the hall, none of the glass fell onto them. It simply splattered straight into the gym, all across the floor, leaving the frame looking naked in the centre. Stephen just stood absolutely still staring straight ahead. It was almost as if he was playing a game of Musical Statues. It seemed to be catching because the others couldn't move either and none of them noticed Mrs Palmer walking towards them. She looked furious. Her face was white and her lips were pursed together in the kind of grimace she always made when she was about to scream into someone's face. She was the kind of teacher they all hated. She never had a good word to say for anyone and they sometimes thought she actually enjoyed it when someone got into trouble.

Flag: Do you think you can always tell how someone is feeling from their body language? Do you think that Mrs Palmer knows how the students feel about her and what they think of her? Do you think this would make any difference to her behaviour if she did know?

Mrs Palmer stood straight in front of them and folded her arms. She was obviously ready to roar into battle. 'Right,' she said, in the kind of voice that shatters glass. 'I want to know who did it and why. Who is the irresponsible person who thinks that kicking a football into a pane of glass is a good idea?' None of you are leaving this playground until I get my answer.'

Kera, Stephen, Alban and Ellen simply looked down. No-one seemed to know what to do at this point.

'I'm waiting,' said Mrs Palmer, 'and I'm sure there will be witnesses if I ask around, so don't attempt to cover up for anyone, will you.'

Stephen stole a sideways glance at Kera. She felt sorry for him – he was going to have to admit to what he'd done but she didn't want him to get into trouble. It didn't seem fair. He hadn't actually meant to break the pane of glass. He simply had a temper and kicked the ball and it seemed as if his temper had manoeuvred its way right through his leg and into his foot. Whatever had happened, that ball had come out with an enormous power. Stephen looked at Mrs Palmer and stared her straight in the eye. For some reason he didn't feel quite so angry anymore. He suddenly felt calmer and he knew what he was going to do.

'It wasn't any one of us,' he said. 'None of us did it, so don't try and accuse us. Some other little twerp came and took the ball and kicked it at that pane of glass. We didn't even see them, but it wasn't any of us so you can just stuff your accusations.'

Ending point: At this point, the following two endings can be read to the students. The facilitator can then ask the students to judge which is the better ending, that is, which one would achieve the best possible outcome for those involved. The students can then be asked to work out the best ending for themselves via the first Circle Time activity listed in the Activities section.

Ending one

Mrs Palmer looked back at Stephen. By this time her face was no longer white – it had turned bright pink. She was obviously absolutely furious.

'I do not expect to be spoken to like that,' she said. 'Not only am I convinced that you are lying to me but you have also now chosen to be extremely rude and aggressive. I'm not having it. Until you agree to come clean, the four of you are in detention and I can assure you that I'm going to ban all of you from the match on Saturday. There's no way that any one of you deserves to play if you cannot even tell the truth about something like this.'

Kera began to say something, 'But Miss, you can't do that. It's really, really important.'

'I should just keep quiet if I were you,' said Mrs Palmer. 'I'm not expecting any responses from any of you from now on. You're coming with me straight away. We're going up to see the head teacher and we're going to sort this out properly. If you won't tell me the truth then you can tell him the truth and you can stay in detention until you agree to do just that.' No-one said anything and no-one looked at each other at this point. I just wish Stephen would tell the truth, thought Kera. If he'd just say something, if he'd just apologise, it might make a bit of a difference. We might be able to salvage the situation.

Stephen looked across at her. It was almost as if he knew what she was thinking.

'Don't even go there,' he said under his breath. 'There is no way I'm getting into trouble for this. It's all your fault. You lot made me angry. You made me do it.'

'Don't be ridiculous,' said Alban. 'You're acting like a total prat!'

'Oh well, if that's what you think,' said Stephen. 'Just tell on me then. Go on, be a grass if that's what you're going to be. You idiot.'

Alban couldn't stop himself at that point. He saw red. There was no way that he could handle being called a grass – Kera knew it. She tried to hold him back but it was too late. He'd turned round and before anyone could stop him he had punched Stephen directly on the face. Mrs Palmer looked round and screamed. It wasn't just a lie any more, thought Kera. This was going to be even more serious.

Ending two

Mrs Palmer's face was a picture. She was obviously absolutely furious.

'I don't think I saw who did that,' she said. 'But I'm absolutely certain it was one of you. The ball came from this direction – there's no-one else on the football pitch so who could it have been? Now, come on – come clean.'

Kera and Ellen looked at each other. Stephen and Alban both looked at their feet.

What is it about boys sometimes, thought Kera. Why can't they just tell the truth? Why can't they admit it when they have done something wrong?

'I'm waiting,' said Mrs Palmer, 'and I'm not prepared to wait for much longer. Come on, out with it.'

Alban continued to look at his feet. He was looking very white and very strained. He could feel himself beginning to panic. He didn't want any of them to miss the match on Saturday. He certainly did not want to miss it but he knew that the smashed pane of glass cost a lot of money and it might cost them the match as well. Almost without thinking he lifted his head and said, 'I did it, I did it, it was me Miss, I'm sorry Miss, it was an accident Miss, I'm really sorry. I couldn't help it, I just kicked the ball and for some reason it went in the wrong direction. I couldn't help it Miss – honest.'

'Right,' said Mrs Palmer. 'In now. We're going straight to the head teacher's office and he'll deal with you.' The others watched in amazement as Alban marched behind Mrs Palmer back into the main school building. Kera and Ellen both looked at Stephen. For one moment he appeared to be speechless. Then he turned round and smiled. 'Well, that's alright then,' he said. 'At least we'll be able to play in the match. Alban can have a rest this weekend, don't you think?' Kera couldn't help herself.

'You're awful,' she said. 'How could you let him do that?'

'Well, it's up to him,' said Stephen. 'If he wants to act like a prat, let him act like a prat. I don't care. I'm not losing the match. I'll be 'Man of the Match' again, that's for sure.'

He walked off, leaving the girls standing staring after him. Neither of them knew what to say. There was nothing to say, or was there?

Activities

Use Circle Time as a vehicle to problem-solve. Ask the students to work out for themselves what would be a better ending to this story. What do they think should have happened and why? What do they think would have been the best thing for each of the characters to have done?

Sometimes we tell a lie almost impulsively just as Alban did in the story. It can be to cover up something that we have done or it can be to protect a friend. It's almost as if we don't stop and think before we open our mouths. The students can consider a time when they may have done this and compare notes within the group.

Sometimes people tell what they call 'white lies' in order to supposedly protect others from hurt or grief. The students can consider when it might be appropriate to tell a white lie. For example, if your friend's recently had a new haircut and it looks ridiculous and they are extremely upset about it, you might say, 'Oh, it's not too bad,' rather than telling them the honest truth which is that it looks awful. You'd probably do this in order to prevent any further hurt or dent their confidence. The students might like to think of a list of times when telling a white lie may or may not be appropriate. Some people may think that telling any lie is never appropriate and this may form part of their belief systems. These ideas can also be discussed in the group.

It may be useful to focus on the question: Does one lie always lead to another?

Work outside school

People are very often cynical about politicians and the way they behave and seemingly fail to meet the promises they make at election times. The students may wish to investigate the performance of their local or national politicians by referring back to previous election pledges. How many of these have they met? Why haven't they met them? Have they lied? If so, why? Do people in public life often lie and, if so, do they do this knowingly or are they simply fed false information? For example, Tony Blair seemed to think that he was fed inaccurate information during the Iraq war. The students could compile mini dossiers on relevant political figures and present these in the form of newspaper reports.

Reflection

The students may wish to reflect upon what the world might be like if people never told lies. Would it really be a Utopia? Would it be perfect or would people get hurt and upset by each other's lack of sensitivity and caring? Sometimes the truth can be very, very hard to bear. For example, someone who has been diagnosed with a terminal illness may not wish to acknowledge this fact right up until the point at which they actually die. Is this their choice or should they be made to confront the truth? There are obviously big lies and little lies. Do these little ones always result in bigger ones being told and developed? How can we be as honest as we can without hurting other people? This is an ethical dilemma for many of us and the students may wish to reflect on their own behaviours and to particularly focus on how they would feel if they are lied to and how they would feel when they lie to others.

Session 3: No Difference Allowed

Focus

- awareness of difference and acceptance of diversity

- consideration of other's feelings and empathy

- understanding of how different values can cause conflict

- using brain and feelings to uniform behaviour

- understanding how we can develop our own value system which enables us to make our own decisions.

This story is about the ways in which one group of children find it both easy and difficult to welcome a new boy into their peer group. One child has a particularly difficult time in accepting that his friends do not feel the same way as he does. He also has to cope with a growing awareness that his family's views and belief systems are very different to those of his peers. There is a conflict between the two systems, which causes some stress alongside raising awareness of the need to develop a personal set of values and beliefs.

Either stop the story and discuss the Flag points as you read or read the whole story and use these as discussion points prior to completing the activities.

Adil was looking forward to starting his new school even though he was feeling quite nervous about meeting so many new people. He'd moved from Bradford down to South London with his family because his dad's job had been relocated. He knew that this wasn't easy for any of them. His mum was really upset as she'd miss her friends and family. She said it was much harder for her to make the move than anyone else in the family because she wouldn't be able to go out and meet new people so easily. It would be difficult to make new friends if you basically spent most of your time in the house looking after the family. Adil felt sorry for his mum but that was simply what it was like for a lot of mums in their community. Anyway, he was sure that she'd eventually meet other Muslim women though the group at the Mosque. Of course it would be difficult at first, but she'd get used to it.

Flag: Why do people get nervous about meeting new people or going into a new situation? Do you think that everybody feels this way? Why does Adil think that it is harder for women in his community to make new friends? What do you think about this?

Anyway, Adil's new school was literally two minutes walk from their new home, which was ideal considering the fact that he always had to be dragged out of his bed in the morning. He'd always hated getting up and it had always been the cause of major rows with his mum and dad and his three elder sisters. It now looked like things would improve in this respect at least as he could wait until at least 8:25am before taking his turn in the bathroom, by which time they'd all be finished and off to work. So at least he'd have a nag-free shower time, breakfast time and walk to school. When he did eventually get to the main gates on that first day, he was feeling a real mixture of emotions. He looked around at all the other kids going through the gates. They all seemed to be quite relaxed. There were a few bits of play fighting going on but nothing major. What was interesting was that the majority of the students were white. In fact, he'd only counted two Asian girls, two Turkish boys and an Afro-Caribbean girl in the whole time he'd been standing at the gate. It made him feel a bit odd – not scarred – just a bit uncomfortable and he didn't really know why that should be the case.

Flag: What kind of emotions do you think Adil would have been experiencing on his first day? Have you ever walked into a totally 'new' situation and did you experience these kinds of feelings? Why would the fact that most of the students were white cause Adil to feel uncomfortable? What do you think they may have been thinking or feeling about him as they saw him watching them?

The bell went and everyone rushed into the main building. He knew he'd have to go straight to the head teacher's room as that had been arranged earlier by his mum and dad as neither of them were able to go with him on his first day. After a brief welcome meeting, Adil found himself being rushed through the corridors towards his first room. The head teacher apologised for not spending longer with him but she had a very important meeting to go to and needed to leave the building by 9:15am. Adil didn't mind. He was just keen to get into the classroom – to get that awkward bit over with when you first walk through the door and meet all of those new faces. He took a deep breath and walked in after the head teacher. The next half an hour felt like a total blur when he thought about it later. He remembered seeing a sea of faces and being given a seat next to a girl called Carmel. She smiled at him and asked him his name straight away. That's when he first felt it. It was at that moment when Joseph who was sitting directly in front of him turned around and gave him 'the look'. The one that says, 'You're different – I don't like you – you're not allowed here.'

Flag: How would you make someone feel welcome into your class group? What does Adil mean by 'the look' and how can he be sure that he's got this right? How would this have made you feel if you were in his shoes?

It was later on at lunchtime that Adil had his suspicions confirmed. The Form Tutor, Mr Henry had arranged for Carmel and Dean to look after Adil on his first day. So they'd shown him around the main buildings and taken him into the dining hall. It was self-service which Adil was grateful for, as most of the food was, in his opinion, inedible – mainly fatty and fried foods with very few fresh vegetables. He had a real job selecting anything suitable from what was on offer. He eventually ended up with a plate of limp lettuce leaves, green beans and rice. It was when he sat down that it all really began. Joseph sat down directly opposite him. He looked at Adil's plate and then said, 'What's that? Don't you eat real food?' Adil looked at him blankly.

'Sorry?' he asked.

'I said – don't you eat meat? What's wrong with you? Why haven't you got some proper food on your plate?'

Carmel pulled a face at Joseph. 'Just shut up you idiot. He's a vegetarian, probably.'

'Anyway,' said Dean, 'Muslims don't eat pork do you Adil?'

Adil nodded. He was amazed that Joseph had been so rude. His mum and Dad would say that this was really insolent behaviour. Joseph wasn't deterred and continued.

'Yeah, Muslims don't eat meat – just like they don't wash on Sundays, but beat their wives and treat them like slaves. That's what my dad says. He says people like you shouldn't be allowed into this country. You should go back to where you belong.'

'Yeah and we all know that your dad's just a racist idiot so you can stop spouting his views. We don't need to hear all that rubbish here,' said Dean

'And you should know better anyway,' said Carmel. 'You know we've got rules about all of that here – we agreed those together in the school – so unless you want me to report you, you should just take all of those things back and apologise.'

Adil looked absolutely stunned. He couldn't believe they were having this conversation. He'd never experienced anything like it. He thought that was probably because everyone in his school in Bradford had been Asian so the argument just never came up. It just wasn't an issue. They were just all the same.

Ending point: At this point, the following two endings can be read to the students. The facilitator can then ask the students to judge which is the better ending, that is, which one would achieve the best possible outcome for those involved. The students can then be asked to work out the best ending for themselves via the first Circle Time activity listed in the Activities section.

Ending one

Adil took a deep breath. He looked directly at Joseph.

'Look,' he said, 'I don't want any bother. If you feel like that then just keep away from me and I'll keep away from you. If you can't change how you feel or think then you'll never be comfortable with me. I am the way I am and I'm proud of it. I don't think you're any worse or better than me but your acting like an idiot now so I really don't want to be around you!'

He then got out of his seat, picked up his lunch tray and walked over to another table at the opposite end of the dining hall. Carmel looked in disgust at Joseph.

'Now look what you've done – you really are a prat.'

'Yeah – a stupid prat,' said Dean.

'Oh shut up you pair of Paki lovers,' Joseph said raising his voice.

'You're pathetic,' said Carmel. 'If you want everyone to know you're a racist idiot that's fine but I don't want to be associated with you either.' She picked up her tray and walked across the room to sit down next to Adil.

'I suppose you're going to clear off next then?' Joseph said to Dean.

'No – I've just about finished my lunch, but I'm going to give you a bit of advice. Just because your dad's a member of the BNP and thinks like that, it doesn't mean that you have to think like that. You know that what you said earlier about Muslims is just a load of rubbish – you just think that's what you should say or maybe you're so scared of your dad that you can't say what you really think. It's like he won't let you. Just think about it – that's all I'm saying.'

With that, Dean also stood up and walked away from the table.

Joseph looked puzzled. He shrugged his shoulders and continued to eat his lunch but he felt uncomfortable. He liked Dean and Carmel. They were his mates, or at least he thought they were until now. He hadn't realised what they really thought of his dad. 'But they must have thought I was OK or they'd have said something by now, wouldn't they?'

Ending two

Joseph looked uncomfortable. He knew that his face was bright red. Carmel and Dean had never talked to him like that before. He'd always thought they were good mates – but not now. At this point in time he felt like slapping them. He clenched his fist and took a deep breath. Carmel sighed.

'Look, I know that was tough – but don't you see, you can't say stuff like that. It's just not right and it's not fair.'

'We know you get brainwashed by your old man but he's wrong. You know he is, we've had this conversation before so many times,' said Dean.

Adil looked really upset. He couldn't believe they were having this conversation. The atmosphere was electric – like at any moment there would be an explosion – what of he wasn't sure.

'Yeah – but I don't think my dad's all wrong you know.' Joseph was beginning to look really uncomfortable. On the one hand he liked his friends and he didn't mind that they liked black people. He just didn't want to be forced into sharing their views. He couldn't. He couldn't go against his dad and he couldn't say his dad was all wrong either. When you love someone, it's difficult. 'Even if they do something wrong, you wouldn't grass them up, would you?' he thought. Adil looked at Joseph.

'It's OK,' he said. 'I know it's hard. My dad's similar. He doesn't like people who aren't Muslim. He says that they all rot in hell and they're all unclean but I don't agree with him. I've never really had any non-Muslim mates, mainly because everyone was the same at my old school. No-one was different but I think I can accept it if someone is. I just wouldn't say a lot about it to my dad as he'd be likely to have a fit. He reckons we should just keep ourselves to ourselves and work hard, especially at school. I think it's hard though as I'd like to have some mates here even if they are different to me.'

Carmel smiled at him. 'You will have mates – no worries there. Just be yourself. We're not racist are we?' She turned to the others. Dean smiled but Joseph looked down at his feet. He said nothing then he walked away.

Activities

Use Circle Time as a vehicle to problem-solve. What do they think would have been a better ending to this story? How could both Adil and Joseph have had a better outcome? What needed to happen or change and how?

Being or feeling 'different' in some way is not always easy. The students can brainstorm as many differences as they can think of and then consider what would help each individual to feel more included and less different . For example, race, language, physical/ sensory disability, religion, sexuality and politics.

Students can consider how easy or difficult it would be to hold one set of views or values and yet be expected to live and behave in a totally contrary way in another context, that is, at school or work. What sort of stresses and dilemmas would arise? Do they know of people who have or haven't coped in such situations? What happened and why?

Work outside school

Ask the students to act as 'reporters'. Their task is to interview a member of their own family or local community and to formulate a series of questions around the topic of 'difference'. These may include:

- A focus on what made that individual feel, look or behave differently in different contexts.
- What feeling 'different' actually 'felt' like?
- How others reacted to them and why they think they did so in this way.
- How they did (or didn't) manage to find a way of living within a world in which they knew themselves to be different.

Students can present these in the form of a magazine interview with questions, answers and illustrations and make use of a digital camera and perhaps photographs provided by the interviewee.

Reflection

Ask the students to put themselves in someone else's shoes. What would it feel like to have been a young Jewish child growing up in Nazi Germany? What would it feel like to be a refugee from Rwanda coming into this country after seeing your parents butchered in front of your eyes?

They can consider the nature of discrimination and racism. Why does it happen? Where does it come from? Is it ever justified and if not, why not? Do we all need to think in the same way? What sort of world would it be if we did?

How can we make our own communities inclusive? What do we really mean by this term?

Session 4: Labelled

Focus

‣ awareness and acceptance of difference

‣ difficulties in labelling others and self

‣ using brain and feelings to inform reactions to others

‣ understanding the importance of expressing feelings to others in order to resolve conflicts and problems

‣ developing assertive behaviours in order to achieve healthier and more positive outcomes.

This story is about the ways in which one child responds to the labels he has been given by both his parents and other children. He is the third child in the family and his elder two siblings are both girls who have been regarded as high achievers. They have always been 'top of the class' and gained a series of 'A' grades in all academic assessments undertaken to date. This has been particularly difficult for Jason who is still struggling in Year 7 to master his basic skills. His mum has decided that he's just not very bright and continually tells him not to worry about this, as she's not expecting him to become a brain surgeon. Jason faces such labelling in both the home and the school context and begins to feel a real sense of injustice and anger which leads to some aggressive responses. When asked to reflect upon his behaviours and choices he is prompted to consider how he might react differently and how others might react differently to him, particularly if he chooses to adopt more assertive responses.

Either stop the story and discuss the Flag points as you read or read the whole story and use these as discussion points prior to completing the activities.

Jason was fed up. He was so fed up that he really didn't want to go home. He spent at least an hour making what would usually be a ten minute walk to his home from school. As he went, he kicked his football into the side of the pavement repeatedly – almost as if he thought he could actually crack it open. It was the end of his first week at secondary school and he just hated it.

He hated everything about it – having to move around from room to room for every lesson, having to sit down for a whole 50 minute session and pretend to listen to the teacher and having to attempt to copy stuff from the board which he just couldn't do. He just couldn't get the words down on the paper fast enough so, at the end of the week, he hadn't been able to do one piece of homework properly because he didn't get enough time to actually write the task down before the bell went for the next lesson. He really felt as though he'd had enough. He just wanted to be back in his old school – not because he was soft – but simply because he knew what he had to do there and the teachers seemed to know how to help him so he didn't feel thick. 'Here they just make me feel like an idiot,' he thought, 'but then that's just what everyone at home thinks I am anyway so what does it matter?'

Flag: Why is coping with change difficult for many of us? Do you think that many students would feel like Jason during their first few weeks at a new school? How do you think his feelings are impacting upon his behaviours at this point?

When he eventually got home, Jason crept round to the back of the house. He was hoping to avoid his mum. Every night this week she'd given him the third degree as soon as he'd walked in.

'Well – how did it go? What did you do? What was the work like?' and worst of all, 'And what homework have you got?' It was the last question that finished him off. He just wanted to shout at her, 'I don't know! I'm so dim I didn't get to write it down – OK?' But he didn't say that of course. He just lied and said he didn't have any or that he'd left the sheet at school and would bring it home tomorrow and do it at lunchtime. He told her that the teachers had said they wouldn't be giving them much homework for the first couple of weeks anyway because they knew it was hard having to cope with so many changes. He lied. It was simply easier that way.

Flag: What do you think about this lying? What would you have done in this situation? Is it always wrong to lie or do we sometimes need to resort to 'white' lies in order to protect ourselves or others? Had this behaviour become a habit for Jason?

He turned the corner and went up to the back door which suddenly opened – almost as if by magic. His mum was standing there, her arms folded and her face rather pink. He knew that look. She'd definitely rumbled him and was about to have her usual quiet explosion.

'Go and sit down at the table Jason,' she said. 'I've made you a cup of tea. I think we need to talk.'

'What about, Mum?' he asked.

'You – your school – what's really been going on?'

'What do you mean, what's really been going on?' he asked. She looked at him and sighed. The explosion had obviously been deferred. She was now back in aggrieved mode. Jason sighed inwardly. At least this was a bit safer. 'Look, I spoke to your form tutor today. She said they were worried about you at school. Apparently, you've not been doing your work. You've not given in one piece of homework and in the lessons you just look a bit spaced out to them. In fact, they've asked my permission to put you on their Special Needs register as they think you might have learning difficulties. I told them that's what I thought too, so they're going to try and get you sorted out with some more help.'

'What?' said Jason. He'd turned purple. This was the final straw. They'd all ganged up on him now. 'You mean you all think I'm dumb – just because I'm not as good as Gemma and Alison. It's not fair!' he said.

'No, that's not it,' his mum said. She looked really upset. She took a deep breath and continued. 'Look, we're only all concerned about you. We just want you to get the help that you need so you can be happier and do better at school – that's all.'

'No, you don't!' Jason was really shouting by now. 'You all just want to write me off and say I'm dumb. I'm not dumb – I'm not!'

'But you do find all the reading and writing stuff difficult – you know that – you always have done. Ever since you went into Mrs Pritchard's class in Reception we knew you needed a bit more help. You didn't pick things up quickly like your sisters. I mean, they were reading fluently by the time they got into Year 1. Then, of course, you have to have the speech and language therapy and you know I've always been convinced that your speech held you back. That's what the therapist said. She was convinced you were dyslexic and so was Mrs Pritchard. It was only that silly old educational psychologist woman that didn't agree and thought she knew better. Otherwise, we could have got more help for you back then and you might have got better than you are now.'

Jason put his hands over his ears. He stood up and walked over to his mum. Then he shouted directly into her face, 'Just shut up! Shut up! I don't want to hear anymore of it!'

Flag: People are often worried about others if they genuinely care for them and want the best for them. Do you think this is the line of Jason's mum? Do you think Jason understands his mum's perspective? Does his mum really understand how he feels? Why do people sometimes become aggressive when they feel misunderstood or labelled?

His mum looked shocked. She'd never thought of Jason as being aggressive. Perhaps his problems at school were making him feel so bad that his behaviour would now really deteriorate, she thought to herself. She held on to the side of the table, realising that she actually felt quite shocked. She didn't know what to say to him but that didn't matter. He obviously didn't want to talk. He simply pushed past her and thundered up the stairs, banging his bedroom door behind him.

Ending point: At this point, the following two endings can be read to the students. The facilitator can then ask the students to judge which is the better ending, that is, which one would achieve the best possible outcome for those involved. The students can then be asked to work out the best ending for themselves via the first Circle Time activity listed in the Activities section.

Ending one

Jason's mum took a deep breath. She sat down at the table and stared at her cup of tea. She didn't feel like drinking it now. She just felt drained of all energy. She really loved her son. He'd been a total surprise coming seven years after his two sisters and she'd always called him the little 'runt' of the family. He was such a tiny baby, she thought. I suppose we all babied him. The girls just treated him like their little baby boy toy. She walked across to the kettle and put it on to boil again.

Just then the kitchen door slowly opened. She looked round and saw Jason standing there. He looked calmer but his eyes were bright red. She smiled lamely at him.

'Do you fancy a fresh cup of tea?' she asked. He nodded and sat down at the table. His mum made the tea and put a mug in front of him.

'Thanks,' he said. 'Look Mum, I'm sorry I got so mad at you – but I'd just had enough. All week I've felt angry at school because everything was so rushed and I couldn't keep up. I just felt even more angry because it's like you and the teachers now seem to be saying it's my fault when I know it's not. It just hurts when you say I'm dumb.'

'But I never said that,' she interjected.

'But you nearly did and I felt like you did. It just gets me down. You're always saying how clever the girls are and how I never did as good as them – it makes me want to lash out. You're my mum – aren't mums supposed to think you're brilliant all the time and not say you're dumb?'

'That's not what I said – I'm just sorry you felt it. I wish you'd told me how you'd been feeling before. I could have done something to help rather than carried on making you feel like this,' she said.

'Mum, I couldn't say. I was just so angry with you and with the teachers. It was like no-one was going to listen to me anyway and that they'd all just labelled me a dumbo,' he said.

His mum smiled. 'Well, let's put our heads together and have a think – it seems like I need to be listening to you rather than listening to me a bit more, don't you think?' They both laughed and sat in silence for a few moments. There was no rush to speak now. After all, maybe thinking and listening were better options at this moment, don't you think?

Ending two

Jason's mum looked shocked. She couldn't ever remember him speaking to her in quite such an aggressive tone. It just wasn't like him. He was always such a placid and quiet little boy – slow and calm – those were the words she'd use to describe him, she thought. Then she suddenly took a deep breath. 'Oh no,' she said aloud. It was as if, in that moment, she suddenly realised what she had done. I've just done it again, she thought. I've given him another few labels, I've just gone and done it again.

She decided to go up to Jason's room and try to have a chat with him. She didn't quite know what she was going to say but she was determined to sort this out. She knocked on his door. There was silence. She tried again. 'Jason – please let me in, love,' she said. 'We need to talk. I don't want you being upset and stressed out like this. It's making me feel bad too,' she said. Jason was sitting on his bed his fists clenched. He was still furious with his mum and with everyone else in his life at that moment in time. But he knew this would have to get sorted. It was time for him to take charge.

He stood up and opened the door. His mum looked really upset but he didn't feel that sorry for her.

She shouldn't be so stupid, he thought. What he didn't realise was that he'd said it out loud. His mum gasped.

'That's not a nice thing to say.'

'No,' Jason said, 'and neither is saying I'm dumb and comparing me to my sisters all the time. If I need some help then you should be helping me – not slagging me off, so go and sort it out mum. I'm too angry to talk to you now.'

He turned his back on his mum. She shook her head but knew she'd no option. She left the room, quietly closing the door behind her.

Activities

Use Circle Time as a vehicle to problem-solve. Discuss the two endings and ask them to consider which would achieve the best outcome for Jason and his mum. What would they suggest? How would they encourage both characters to see each other's perspectives? How could Jason and his mum help and effectively support each other and themselves?

Students can consider how 'labels' can be helpful or unhelpful, drawing up lists of both categories and giving reasons as to why they think the labels would be positive or negative for the individuals or groups concerned. They may wish to create a third category – unhelpful and helpful.

It may be helpful to brainstorm the question: How could we prevent negative labelling in our school community? The students can consider the kinds of rules, regulations, behaviour and policy that they would like to see. They may wish to develop a questionnaire to ask others. For example, teaching staff, support staff, parents and carers, other students, lunchtime staff and cleaning staff can give their views and input.

Work outside school

It may be useful for students to ask their parents or carers about their own experiences of being labelled or seeing others being labelled. How did they feel about this? What happened? How do they feel this experience impacted upon them or those they observed? This discussion could be structured by using a questionnaire which could also raise other questions such as: What do you think about stereotyping others? When do you think 'labels' can be positive?

Reflection

Ask the students to consider how they might feel and behave in a range of situations. What would be happening in their heart (feelings), head (thinking) and body (acting) if they were given the following labels by others: dumb, racist, skinny, aggressive, a mouse, overweight, boffin, sexy, a bully, or disabled.

Students can be encouraged to consider their personal responses first and then share these with a partner or in a smaller group, identifying similarities and differences in their responses. How can we reject negative labels in an assertive way? Can we stop ourselves from labelling others and should we? Why do we generally need to protect our self-esteem and the self-esteem of those we care for? Is putting others down or negatively labelling them helpful in maintaining our own self-esteem? If so, why? Is this right?

Session 5: Getting Justice

Focus

▶ awareness of the concepts of fairness and justice

▶ using brain and feelings to inform behaviours

▶ planning actions and responses as opposed to reacting

▶ distinguishing between assertive and aggressive behaviours

▶ understanding further the concept of 'power' in relationships

▶ distinguishing between vengeance and justice.

This story is about a group of children who are wrongly accused by a teacher of stealing money collected for a trip. They just happen to be in the wrong place at the wrong time, that is, in the classroom at break time when the money appears to have gone missing. As the teacher is only aware of their presence in the classroom at this time and no-one else seems to have witnessed any other 'culprits', it is naturally assumed that they are to blame. This results in a real sense of injustice and powerlessness and the group have to make choices about how they respond – particularly given the fact that they are not themselves in any kind of powerful position. Concepts of truth, justice and fairness all arise, as does the need to self-reflect and plan responses as opposed to merely reacting.

Either stop the story and discuss the Flag points as you read or read the whole story and use these as discussion points prior to completing the activities.

It was the end of the PE session and Year 7 students had been asked to go back to their classrooms to get changed. There was some kind of conference taking place in the gym and things needed to be set up. Most of Callum's form was really pleased about this as it was a freezing day and the thought of having showers was a total turn-off for most of them – including Callum.

'Thank God for that,' he said as they walked down the corridor back to their form room.

'Yeah, but you'll be a real smelly armpit for the rest of the day,' laughed Jarvis. Callum pushed Jarvis and they began to play fight. Just as they reached the door to their form room, Mrs Sparks caught sight of them. She didn't shout. She wasn't that sort of teacher. She just gave them 'the look' – the one that Callum always says lets you know what a silly little idiot you are. It also says 'stop it right now or there'll be big trouble'. The two boys separated themselves and walked into the form room with the rest of their class. There was quite a bit of pushing and shoving alongside lots of laughter. The girls were allowed to go into the stockroom to change, which annoyed quite a few of the boys. Callum, Jarvis and Michael were secretly hoping to embarrass Alison, Michael's twin sister. She knew it and poked her tongue out at them as she went to get changed.

'Better luck next time,' she laughed.

'Right,' said Mrs Sparks, 'Hurry up everyone: you've got exactly two minutes before break. I need to count up and check the trip money so get changed quietly, adding up money is not my strong point.'

She smiled and bent her head over the desk. She piled coins and notes into £10 lots then counted them up, finally writing the total down on a receipt slip before putting everything into her money tin. Just at that point, the break bell went. It was an extremely loud bell and still had the effect of making everyone in the room jump, even though they'd heard it every day for the last two terms. Mrs Sparks quickly put the money box into her desk drawer and walked to the door.

'Come on everyone! Hurry up! The longer you take, the less time you've got! Come on!' she said. Most of the students got changed quickly and made their way out of the classroom. Mrs Sparks was twitching secretly; she was desperate to get down to the smoking room. She was just as keen to get her break as she knew the students were to get theirs. 'God knows what I'll do when they make this a non-smoking environment next term,' she thought, feeling increasingly irritated.

Flag: How would you define 'play fighting'? Is it just a bit of fun or are there potential difficulties in this way of interacting? How do you think teachers can distinguish between this and the real thing? Why do boys and girls at this age need more privacy around their bodies? Is this healthy? Do we need rules to protect our privacy? What do you think of teachers who smoke? Is there any difference between them smoking and young people smoking? Should workplaces all be smoke free? Do smokers have 'rights'?

Five minutes had gone by and Mrs Sparks knew she'd just have to leave them to it. There was no other way if she was going to manage to make a cup of coffee and have a quick fag before the next lesson. She quickly looked round the room. Alison walked through into the classroom from the stockroom. She laughed at Callum, Jarvis and Michael. Two of them still hadn't got their shoes and socks on.

'It's OK, Miss,' she said, 'you go – we'll make sure we shut the door. I'll get these three out in just a minute – no worries.'

Mrs Sparks smiled. She liked Alison – she was like a little old woman – just a small girl but with an adult's head on those narrow shoulders. She always got the jokes she told – even when they seemed to go way above the heads of the majority of the kids in the class. Also, she knew when to have a laugh and when to draw the line and stop, which was unusual for a kid of 11 or 12 years. 'Still, she's more like 11 going on 31,' she thought as she hurried up the corridor into the staff room.

Flag: What do you think it is about Alison that Mrs Sparks really likes? How do you know if a teacher does or doesn't like you? How do you think they know if you like or don't like them? Do you think liking or disliking the adults who have responsibility for you is important? How would you describe the perfect teacher from your perspective? How do you think the teacher would describe the perfect pupil? Would they have characteristics in common?

Alison turned round to look at the boys. She smiled wearily.

'Come on,' she said, 'We've only got about eight minutes left and I want to go to the tuck shop!'

'Alright – keep your hair on,' said Michael. 'Anyway, do you really think you ought to be buying stuff from the tuck shop? You're looking quite podgy, you know.'

'Yeah, you'll soon be doughnut sized if you carry on stuffing in all those Mars bars and crisps,' said Jarvis.

'Oh shut up! As if I care what you lot think anyway!' shouted Alison. With that, she ran out of the room.

'Well, you've blown it there,' said Callum. 'She won't talk to you for a week now – you know what girls are like for sulking.' Jarvis shrugged his shoulders trying to look as if he didn't care but his face was red. As soon as he'd said it he realised he'd made a mistake. 'There was joking and there was joking,' his mum always said, 'and you always take the joke too far Jarvis – too near the knuckle!'

'Come on,' he said to the others. 'Let's go.' All three boys ran out of the room and into the playground determined to get at least the last few minutes in on the football pitch.

Flag: Why do you think Alison reacted as she did to Jarvis' comments? Words often hurt a great deal more than physical aggression – why do you think this is? Is it always possible to know if a joke has gone 'too far'? Can we see the warning signs in others' reactions before we take things to this level? When do you think teasing becomes bullying?

When they got back into their form room after break, everyone knew that something was really wrong. They knew it as soon as they saw Mrs Sparks. No-one had ever seen her look quite so pink and straight-lipped before. It was almost as if her lips were iced together. People seemed to feel the icy atmosphere as soon as they came into the room. Rather than the usual jostling, laughing and pushing, there was a strange sense of calm about everyone and everything. Everyone seemed to go to their seats in a robotic fashion and sat down without even being directed to do so.

Mrs Sparks cleared her throat. 'I feel – well – quite shocked,' she said. 'I'm afraid that when we were at break the money for the trip was stolen. It was just over £300 in coins and notes. I left the money box in my desk drawer. I didn't lock it because I was rushed and forgot. Anyway, I should have thought that I could trust all of you lot by now.' She stopped and looked around the room. There was absolute silence. Then she looked directly over to where Callum, Jarvis, Michael and Alison were sitting.

'Well, I'm afraid to say that when I left the room there were only four of you remaining. Mr Hurst was on duty at the end of the corridor. He saw Callum, Michael and Jarvis come out of the room just after Alison. No-one else came out and apparently no-one else went in. So, unfortunately for all of us, I can only assume that you are the prime suspects here. No-one else was near the room and you all saw where I'd put the money box. I'm afraid I'm going to have to ask all four of you to go straight to the Head's office now. You can tell him what you know and I just hope you've all got the sense to be truthful!'

'B...b...but it wasn't us! That's not fair!' shouted Jarvis.

'Miss, we didn't go anywhere near it. We just wouldn't,' said Alison. She was so angry and embarrassed she could hardly get the words out.

'I'm sorry,' said Mrs Sparks, 'but unfortunately all the evidence points to you four. Fairness doesn't come into it. I'm afraid this is a case of guilty until proven innocent.'

 Flag: Can we always tell how people are feeling from their appearance and body language? Why is it sometimes dangerous to assume we can? Are things always as they seem from their appearance? Should people in this kind of situation be presumed guilty until proved innocent? Should it be vice versa? How would you feel if you were one of the students? How do you think the teacher feels? Is she making the 'right' decision? Who has the most and least power here?

 Ending point: At this point, the following two endings can be read to the students. The facilitator can then ask the students to judge which is the better ending, that is, which one would achieve the best possible outcome for those involved. The students can then be asked to work out the best ending for themselves via the first Circle Time activity listed in the Activities section.

Ending one

Jarvis looked astonished. He just couldn't understand how Mrs Sparks could be so unfair and such a liar. He shook his head in disbelief.

'You haven't got one bit of proof, anyone else could have crept in without being seen.'

'Look,' said Mrs Sparks in a weary voice, 'I'm not going to get into a discussion about this with you. I've got a lesson to teach. Mr Burford is waiting for you in his office. He'll no doubt listen to your explanations.' She turned away and began to write on the whiteboard behind her.

'Mr Burford can just bugger off. He's not a judge and I'm not taking this from you!' shouted Jarvis.

Alison and Callum both looked at him as if they were about to approach him and try to stop him from exploding. But it was too late. He ran across the room, kicking the tables as he went. Alison, Callum and Michael ran after him. Mrs Sparks looked up and asked another pupil to shut the door. She felt relieved they'd gone out of the room and just hoped they'd have the sense to get themselves to the Head's office.

Callum ran after Jarvis and grabbed hold of his arm.

'Come on, mate. Look, we'll get our chance to tell the truth. Come on, get a grip,' he said. Jarvis looked at him.

'You don't get it, do you? There was no-one else in the room – no-one saw anyone else go in so they definitely have us marked for it. She has anyway and let's face it, if the teacher says it was us – that's what everyone will believe.'

'Yeah, everyone always believes the adult and never the kid,' said Michael, looking totally fed up.

'Well, I'm not standing for it. We'll get our own back. If she's going to accuse us of doing something we didn't do, then we'll really go and do something!' said Jarvis.

'Don't be an idiot!' said Alison. 'We've got no choice. We've got to go and see Mr Burford.'

'Well, you can. I'm not. Make your choice, you can come with me and seriously damage Sparkies' new motor or go and creep to Burford.'

'You're mad,' said Alison.

'Definitely,' said Callum. 'That's just going too far. Come on, let's go back in.'

Callum moved towards the door and Alison and Michael followed. Jarvis watched them for what seemed like seconds. He'd made his mind up. There was no justice in this world. He'd need to make his own.

Ending two

'There's no proof at all,' said Jarvis, thinking aloud. 'You can't think it was us Miss – you can't.' Mrs Sparks looked directly at Jarvis.

'Look, just go and talk to the Head. You know he'll listen. I've got a lesson to teach now so I can't talk to you. Please, all of you go now.'

They left the room and, in silence, made their way to the Head's office.

They were too shocked and stunned to discuss it for the first few minutes. Then Alison said, 'Look, I've got to ask this but, you know I left the room before you guys – you…um…didn't…' her voice trailed off.

'What are you on about Al? What are you saying? You should know we wouldn't. You know we're not that sort. We might do the odd shop but not something big like this – you know that!' Alison grinned. She looked relieved. 'Sorry. I just had to ask.'

'Exactly, like they will and like you they won't be able to help themselves – we'll definitely be guilty,' said Jarvis.

'I'm not so sure,' said Alison. 'I've just been thinking, I was getting changed in the stock room and I'm pretty sure I heard something or someone messing around behind the boxes at the back as I left the room. I'm not absolutely sure but it would make sense, wouldn't it?'

'Yeah look, we need to stay calm about this and use our brains rather than get worked up. Right, Jarvis?' asked Callum. Jarvis nodded.

'At least he's listening now,' thought Callum.

'We need to tell Mr Burford that and just say what we did, or rather didn't, do,' said Michael. 'If we can put any doubt in his mind – which I think we can – then that should help us get out of this.'

'I hope so,' said Jarvis. 'Look, you do the talking Callum – you're the calmest and I'll just get aggressive again. I can feel it!'

'OK, so we'll just tell the truth. That's all we can do. I'll talk and tell him about the noise Al heard. Let's hope it works.'

The door to the Head's room suddenly opened and Mr Burford quietly asked them to come in. They walked into the room and waited.

Activities

Use Circle Time as a vehicle to problem-solve. Discuss the two endings and ask the students to consider which (if any) would achieve the better outcome for the students involved. What do they think the students should do? How can they get justice for themselves in what seems like a very difficult situation?

Students can consider times when there have been miscarriages of justice. For example, those accused of IRA bombings or of killing their babies. What must it have felt like to lose your liberty and reputation? What effects did these miscarriages of justice have on the rest of the family?

Students can brainstorm the question: If you can't get justice, should you resort to getting vengeance? They can consider a range of situations when it may not be possible to get justice because (as in the story) the circumstantial evidence seems so great. They can work in small groups and feed back to the group as a whole.

Students can role-play assertive and aggressive responses to a range of situations in which someone is accused wrongly of doing something by a teacher or adult:

- cheating in a test
- talking in class
- stealing some money
- two timing
- smoking/taking drugs
- fighting.

They can be encouraged to formulate their response scripts and to focus on the importance of engaging the brain prior to reacting.

Work outside school

Students can research the Criminal Justice System. How did it come about? How does it work? What are the processes and procedures and who is involved? They may wish to compile information sheets which explain how people get to court, what happens and who is involved at each stage.

Reflection

Students can consider whether or not the concept of fairness is useful. Is life fair? For example, is it fair for someone who is considered to be a 'good' person to get a terminal illness such as terminal cancer? Is it fair that people are starving or the objects of terrorism? Can the world be made a fairer place? What can we, as individuals, do? What can we do collectively? When would we feel the need to get vengeance? Would this happen after the sexual abuse of our child, a murder or a rape of someone close to us? How do we feel about people who commit such crimes and how would we react if someone we loved and cared for committed such a crime? Students may also wish to reflect on their own behaviours and reactions. Have they reacted in a negative and unconstructive way when they have been wrongly accused of something? Could they react in a more productive way in the future? If so, how?

Session 6: Bullying

 Focus

- awareness of methods employed to bully others

- understanding and acceptance of others

- awareness of how actions and feelings can affect others

- understanding the consequences of behaviour, thoughts and feelings

- using the brain and feelings to inform behaviour.

This story is about a girl who has just started at her new secondary school. She has entered the school along with several members of her previous Year 6 primary class and consequently initially feels relatively positive and confident about the move. However, she soon begins to realise that these 'old' friends are gradually turning against her and can't quite understand why at first. It later becomes apparent that she doesn't really 'fit in' with their idea of how they'd like to present themselves, that is, she is rather fat and old fashioned in appearance and they are slim and trendy. However, once the group have actually recognised the consequences of their behaviours, they begin to realise that they may not have behaved in a civilised and authentic manner.

Either stop the story and discuss the Flag points as you read or read the whole story and use these as discussion points prior to completing the activities.

Emma and Shakira were standing outside the dining hall waiting for their friends Tammy and Mel. It was Year 7s turn to go in for lunch and both of them were desperate to get some food. They weren't used to having lunch so late. At primary school, everyone went into the hall at 12.00pm and ate at the same time. At secondary school, it was totally different. Everything was staggered as there were simply too many people to sit in on one sitting alone. So today they'd had to wait until 1.20pm.

'I think I'm going to faint if I don't get something to eat soon,' said Emma.

'God, don't be that dramatic. Honestly it's only food, but I do know what you mean,' said Shakira quickly adjusting what she said so as not to hurt her friend. She was hungry too but she didn't think it was really polite to make such a big deal of it. Also, she felt that she shouldn't really be encouraging her friend to think too much of her belly. After all, she was getting bigger almost by the minute. She'd never been skinny like the rest of them but since they'd started at secondary school she just seem to have piled the pounds on.

'Probably nerves,' thought Shakira. After all, it hadn't been easy for most of them having to move from a lovely, small and very cosy primary school to this great big school. There was just so much more to think about all the time and so many different subjects and things to do. It hadn't been easy to get used to.

'Oh, here they are,' said Emma as Tammy and Mel approached. 'Are you ready to go in?'

'You bet,' said Mel grinning. She winked at Tammy.

'You can see Emma's desperate girls, can't you,' she said.

They all laughed – including Emma who hadn't realised the sarcasm in Mel's voice.

Flag: Can we always be honest with our friends? Do you think Shakira could have discussed Emma's weight with her in a helpful way or do you think this would have done more harm than good? Is it always possible to take what people say at face value? Or do they often have alternative agendas? How helpful is sarcasm and why do we use it to put others down?

The girls queued up for their lunch. There was, as usual, a choice of food including chips, nuggets, beans and burgers alongside a few healthier options like three bean salad, vegetarian bake and a range of salads. Most of the students seemed to opt for the less healthy options. Tammy looked down her nose and sniffed as Gary and Craig piled their trays with chicken nuggets and chips.

'No wonder they're both covered in acne and are both getting beer bellies,' she laughed, turning towards Mel.

'What are you having Shakira?' asked Mel.

Shakira was really dying for a big pile of chips and a burger but she saw all three of them turn to her at this point and quickly changed her mind.

'Oh um, I think I'll have a veggie burger and some salad today', she said in a low voice.

'That's good,' said Mel, sounding slightly surprised.

'Still, you need to watch it so it's probably a good idea to go lower carb today. After all, we've got Jo's party to go to next Friday. You want to be able to fit into your best outfit for that, don't you?'

Once again, she winked at the others and went over to sit down at one of the lunch benches. Once they'd all got a seat and began to eat, Tammy began the conversation again.

'Speaking about the party, what are you going to wear?'

'Well, I've got some new satin trousers and this fantastic new top – my mum got it for me last week. It's great. It really clings to your top and waist and then comes out a bit at the bottom so it's almost like a mini-dress. I love it. I just feel so cool in it,' said Mel.

'I bet you look good, it does help having nice long legs though doesn't it? I'm going to wear my new leather jeans and my pink T-shirt – you know, the one with the butterfly on – it's a Versace original. My dad got it for me in the States last month,' said Tammy.

'What about you, Shakira? What are you wearing?' asked Mel.

'Well, I've got everything new! But I'm not telling you yet. You can have a surprise. I'll just give you one clue – my mum says I look just like Posh Spice in it.' She giggled. The girls continued to eat for a few moments. Then Mel spoke again.

'Oops sorry, I forgot to ask about you Emma! What will you be wearing?'

Emma almost choked on her food. She'd actually put too much in her mouth at once almost in an effort to finish what was on her plate quicker than everyone else. She didn't want to be seen to be eating last.

'Oh…um… I'm not sure yet. I think my mum's making me a dress actually.'

The girls giggled.

'Fabulous,' said Mel. 'I'm sure it will be as lovely as the last one.' Tammy almost chocked with laughter whilst Shakira got out of her seat to go back up to the counter to get some fruit. She didn't feel that this was quite as funny as Mel and Tammy did. In fact, she was beginning to feel slightly uncomfortable all round.

Flag: People do sometimes pressure each other into conforming to their way of thinking. What do you think of this? Do you think Emma should have eaten what she wanted to eat? Does it matter if you don't have the 'right' clothes or look? If so, why? If not, why not? Do you think that Emma could have been more assertive? How? What could she have said and done? Would such a change in her behaviour have impacted on the other girl's behaviour?

Once the girls had finished their lunch, they walked out into the playground. Greg and Jamal came up and said hello. They were keen to know who was going to Jo's party. Mel gave them the full list. She was in full flow when Tammy chipped in,

'Oh and don't forget Emma – Miss Little Big One – you know her!' she said laughing.

Jamal looked blankly at her and then smiled.

'Oh yes,' he said, 'I know – the one with the lovely hair and blue eyes,' he said.

'No! Stupid! The fat one! Look, her, over there,' she said pointing to Emma.

'Yeah, exactly,' he said smiling at Emma who looked away blushing.

Mel was laughing out loud but Tammy was furious. She couldn't believe it. How could he fancy a fat cow like Emma when he could be going out with someone as good looking and slim as her? She didn't get it.

Flag: Peoples perceptions of each other can be varied and different. Why was Jamal's reaction to Emma such a shock to Tammy? What had Tammy expected? How do you think she now felt and how did the others perhaps perceive her at this point?

The two boys walked off. Emma didn't know where to look so she just looked down at her feet. Tammy walked straight over to her.

'Just ignore him, Emma. He was only taking the mick out of you,' she said.

'Yeah,' said Mel,' after all, he's really fit and he's only going to go out with someone else who looks good...um...well, not someone with a weight problem. Don't you agree, Shakira?'

'Oh…um…yeah, I suppose so,' she said in reply. Emma could still feel herself blushing. She stood up.

'It's OK. I know he was just teasing. Anyway, I'm going to the toilet. I'll see you in a bit,' she said. She walked off. All she could hear was their laughter as she made her way across the playground.

'We've got to dump her,' said Mel.

'Yeah, she's doing our image some intense damage,' said Tammy.

'I don't know, she's not that bad,' said Shakira.

'Oh don't be a drip. She's out and you know it,' said Tammy.

'I've got an idea, lets just text her. We'll tell her just to keep out of our way, she'll soon get the message,' said Mel.

They weren't aware of the fact that Emma had already got the message. She was, in fact, sitting on the toilet crying quietly as if her heart would break. She felt the mobile phone in her pocket buzzing for the sixth time. Her hand shook as she pulled it out. There was another text message:

'You fat b__ch.'

'Don't come near us again.'

'We don't want you around.'

'Go and lose some blubber.'

'Fat b__ch.'

She knew it was from the girls. She wiped her eyes.

Why? Why are they doing this? she thought. What have I done to them?

She put the phone back into her pocket and walked out of the toilet.

I suppose they're right, she thought. I am just a sad, fat cow with no style and no personality. It's my fault they don't want to hang around with me. I mean, look at me – who would? She felt sick but she kept on walking – out through the school gates, down the road and past the shops. She just walked and walked.

I just don't feel I can breathe, she thought, not realising that she was actually having a panic attack. 'I feel faint…' She stopped still and then she fell, right into the motorbike directly to her right. The driver swerved but it was too late. He'd hit her.

Flag: What do you think of this method of bullying? Do you think the other girls were really aware of the impact it would have on Emma? Why did Emma think this was probably her own fault? If she had a better level of self-esteem would this have helped her to stick up for herself more? Do you think the others would feel any guilt or remorse if they knew what had happened?

Ending point: At this point, the following two endings can be read to the students. The facilitator can then ask the students to judge which is the better ending, that is, which one would achieve the best possible outcome for those involved. The students can then be asked to work out the best ending for themselves via the first Circle Time activity listed in the Activities section.

Ending one

The driver immediately stopped. He was in total distress.

'She just came from nowhere,' he said, 'just nowhere.'

'It's alright,' said a woman who'd witnessed the whole scene 'She fainted and fell into you. There was nothing you could do about it.'

A couple of hours later, Emma was sitting up in bed at the hospital. She'd got two broken ribs, a broken leg and a very bad headache but apart from that she was fine. She wondered how the others were doing and if they knew. What would they be thinking? Then, suddenly, she thought that actually she really didn't care.

It's almost like that knock on the head has brought me to my senses – they're not my mates. They just used me as a punch bag and I was just so soft I put up with it, she thought.

Well, things will be different now. I won't try and be their friend anymore. I'll just be by myself. It'll be a lot easier and less painful. I'd rather have no friends than friends who are not friends, she thought. She smiled lamely to herself. They were tough words and she wasn't really sure if she was that tough. After all, it was lonely being on your own. Just then, she heard someone's voice at the other end of the ward. She recognised that it was Shakira straight away and she could feel herself starting to shake just in that instant. Shakira came up to the bed.

'I'm sorry,' she said holding out a bunch of flowers. 'I hope you'll still be my friend. I didn't really want to join in with it all you know, but I felt scared.'

'Yeah, I know. So did I,' said Emma as she took the flowers.

Ending two

It was a few hours later when the news flew round the school like wildfire. Everyone was talking about Emma's accident.

'Like she suddenly became famous,' said Mel with distaste as the girls walked into their form room.

Everyone had been asked to go back to their forms at the end of the day as the staff were keen to discuss the rumours that had been spreading and to make sure that everyone went home with the right information.

Mr Bunton asked them all to sit down and listen.

'I just need to tell you that Emma is fine. She's suffered a few cuts and bruises and a broken leg. She'll be in hospital until the end of the week so you can all send cards and things until then. However, what we are rather concerned about is why she should have taken off like that in the middle of the school day. It's not like her at all to act in such an impulsive way. We all felt that she's been rather jumpy of late though and just wondered if any of you could shed some light on this?'

The three girls looked down. Shakira could feel her face going bright pink, almost fluorescent. Then Jamal said, 'Well, it might have something to do with her friends, sir. I think they could tell you more.'

'Yeah, a lot more,' added Greg who'd overheard the giggles and comments as Mel and Tammy planned their text messages.

Mr Bunton looked at the girls. Shakira turned away. She felt sick.

'OK, everyone else dismissed. I'll see you three in my office first thing in the morning. I hope that when you all go home tonight you think about things. This is your chance to maybe put a few things right. OK?'

The girls nodded apart from Tammy who just looked furious. I wonder who would be able to put things right and who wouldn't. I'd love to be a fly on the office wall in the morning, wouldn't you?

Activities

Use Circle Time as a vehicle to problem-solve. Discuss the two endings and ask the students which one they prefer and why. Which do they think would be the best for Emma and why? What do they think she should do next? How should she behave when she goes back to school and meets these friends again? What advice would you give her?

Students can draw up a list entitled 'What makes people bully others?' They can brainstorm in smaller groups and then feed back to the class as a whole with the facilitator helping them to identify any similarities or differences in their responses.

Students can draw up an Anti-Bullying Charter and develop their own policy. What processes do they want to include? They may include peer mediation, peer support, bully alerts, counselling, early warning systems and staff and pupil training. Students can also consider the characteristics of the victim. What can be done to help? Who can help and how?

Work outside school

Students can investigate what resources are available to children and teenagers who are experiencing or have experienced bullying. The information could be collated into a display which can then act as a reference to the whole school.

Reflection

Students can self-reflect on their own experiences of either being a bully, being bullied or observing this happening to others. Why did they think this happened? What were the conditions that led to it? Is there anything or anyone that could have prevented it from escalating? Have you ever felt jealous of someone? Why? Could this have led you to be unkind to them? Are adults (parents, carers and teachers) sometimes bullies? Why? How can children cope with this when they are not as powerful?

What would you do now if you knew a friend or relative was being bullied?

Do you think adults experience being bullied like this? Does this make it easier for them to understand when their children are bullied too? Do you think that you don't have to have experienced bullying yourself in order to empathise with someone who has? How would you react now if someone started to bully you? What would you feel, think, say and do? How could you use your brain, feelings, thoughts and behaviours to get a more positive outcome for yourself?

Session 7: Graffiti Gang

Focus

▸ understanding the nature of peer pressure

▸ thinking ahead to the consequences

▸ distinguishing between 'right' and 'wrong' behaviours and the way in which our behaviours impact upon others

▸ understanding how the environment exists for all and the nature of a healthy environment

▸ using both the brain and feelings to inform behaviour.

This story is about a group of children who formulate a gang with the specific intent of creating graffiti in the local environment. They are aware of other such gangs in the area and decide that they need to make their mark by tagging over graffiti produced previously by these gangs. The competition leads to copious amounts of graffiti and a local resident calling the police to report some of the children she'd observed participating in this activity. It is at this point that one member of the group has to make a choice – whether to tell the truth or to lie about their behaviour.

Either stop the story and discuss the Flag points as you read or read the whole story and use these as discussion points prior to completing the activities.

Josh was bored. It was the summer holidays and he just didn't know what he was going to do with all the time. The whole six weeks seemed to span out in front of him like an endless road. He knew that most kids of his age would feel very differently but then they weren't in the same position as him. He was the only one in the family under 20 years of age. His two elder sisters were 20 and 22 years old and both of them worked. So did his mum. That basically meant that he was home alone for the six week holiday with no-one to really talk to or have a laugh with. The other kids he went around with from school lived too far away from him or else they'd gone away for the summer – at least his two best mates were away but then their parents were dead rich and had houses abroad so they were lucky. He wished that his mum was rich and that he could go off to some posh villa in Portugal but she wasn't. There was no money for holidays this year so she'd told him he'd just have to entertain himself.

'I don't know what you're moaning about,' she said. 'After all, you've got the TV, the DVD player and your computer so you should have enough to keep you busy. You kids nowadays are just spoilt. In my day we had none of that stuff and we just went out and made our own fun. What's gone wrong with you lot now? I just don't get it.'

Josh could hear her saying the words in his head. He knew that speech word for word. He'd heard it so many times now.

Flag: Why do you think people generally experience boredom? Do you think Josh's mum really understands how he is feeling? Do you think it is sometimes hard for people to put themselves in others shoes? What sort of 'fun' do you think his mum had when she was his age? Do you think these activities would interest Josh?

Josh went out into the back garden. It was a lovely summer's day and he felt the warmth of the sun on his back.

I just wish I could go for a swim now with Kieran and Ben, he thought. There was an open air pool in the next borough but he didn't fancy going there on his own. He knew that some of the older kids from school would be going and they had a bit of a reputation for bullying the Year 7s and 8s. He didn't want to become another one of their victims. They also had formed what they called 'Graffiti Gangs'. They put a lot of pressure on the younger kids to join the gangs and to participate in what they described as the Graffiti Wars. Each gang would go around trying to cover over each others tags. The gang that was thought to be 'on top' was the one who'd managed to cover over the most area by the end of the school holidays.

Josh had often heard the kids talking about it and planning where they were going to strike next but he never tried to get in on the act. He was actually a brilliant artist and his graffiti would definitely be better than most of the other stuff out there according to his mates. But Josh had always resisted joining one of the gangs. He didn't feel comfortable about some of the places they chose to tag. It was OK if it was somewhere a bit out of the way like under the railway arches but he thought it was a bit much to cover over the front of the old people's home. That just seemed to be a bit over the top to him.

Josh kicked at the side of the garden bench feeling increasingly frustrated with the fact that he had, in his mind, absolutely nothing to do other than swear and think in the sun. He stopped suddenly when he felt his mobile going in his pocket.

'I'd better answer it,' he thought. 'It's probably just Mum doing her usual check-up that I'm not up to any criminal activity.'

But when he did answer the phone, it wasn't his mum at all. It was his twin cousins, Nabil and Amar. They'd phoned to say that their parents had to go over to India for a wedding and would be staying for a month. They had contacted Josh's mum who'd agreed that the two boys could stay with her for the first half of the holidays prior to going to their other Auntie's in Birmingham. Josh was over the moon.

'At last,' he thought. 'Something to relieve the boredom.'

He got on with his two cousins really well. They were both a real laugh – always in trouble for something but you were never bored when you were with them. They knew how to have a good time and weren't afraid of anyone or anything. Their mum had been just the same when she was younger according to Josh's mum. She'd created a mega scandal in the family by marrying an Asian man but as Mum had repeatedly said, it must have been a good choice because they were still together and happy after 20 odd years.

'The same certainly couldn't be said for myself and that father of yours,' she'd said in her usual tirade about men never really growing up or being able to accept responsibilities. Josh always kept quiet when she went on like that. He loved his dad even though he'd dumped them all. Nothing was going to change that, but then nothing was going to change his mum's mind either so it was probably wisest to keep his mouth shut.

Flag: Why would the twins always being in trouble make Josh feel so excited? Why would their mum have caused such a scandal by her actions? What do you think people would object to and why? Is it 'wrong' to marry someone different? How do you think Josh's mum feels about his dad and why would it be difficult for her to understand Josh's feelings?

Anyway, the next day the twins arrived and from that moment on Josh's summer took off. The three boys were never in the house. They were either in the park, at the pool, in the shopping centre or down at the market. It wasn't as if they were doing anything in particular. It was merely the fact that they were with each other. For Josh, it was just being with other people and having a laugh, cussing each other, play fighting and playing their computer games. Josh realised that he'd actually been quite lonely before but he didn't want to admit that in case it made him look soft.

Flag: Why do you think having friends and company is important to us as human beings? Why would Josh look 'soft' if he admitted to feeling lonely? Is it the case that boys find it harder to talk about their feelings than girls? Or is this a myth? What do you think happens when people can't talk about their feelings and keep them bottled up? Is this healthy?

The three boys went on having a good time for the remainder of the first week. It was during the following Monday that things seemed to change. Josh had taken Nabil and Amar to the local shopping centre as he wanted to get some printer paper for the computer. They'd been trying out a new art programme over the weekend and he was desperate to see what some of his drawings looked like. As they turned into the back entrance Nabil noticed the graffiti covering the back wall.

'That's fantastic,' he said stopping to admire the work.

'Yeah,' said Amar. 'It's really good, nearly as good as your stuff Josh.'

Josh had smiled. Then Nabil said, 'Do you know who did it?' Josh answered him and then wished he hadn't. For the rest of that day and for most of the following day Nabil talked about the graffiti gangs. He wanted to know every detail – who was in each gang, their names, their tags, who was the winning gang that week, but most of all, he wanted to know why Josh hadn't joined.

'You could easily have got in – you're a brilliant artist. What's wrong with you mate?'

Josh felt more and more uncomfortable. He liked his cousins but he just felt that they wouldn't understand his reasons. He didn't know why.

Then, Nabil had what he thought was a brilliant idea.

'I know what we'll do.' He said. 'We'll start up our own gang – we'll have our own graffiti gang and we'll out do the lot of them. Best of it is they won't have a clue who's doing it all! It will be like the three invisible Musketeers!'

That's when it had really started. Josh was dragged to every shop they could think of in order to buy all the cans they'd need. They never bought more than One can in any shop as it would have aroused suspicion according to Amar. The following day they'd started in earnest – getting up dead early in order to creep out of the house and begin their graffiti war before anyone else even though of getting out of bed.

Josh went along with it. He'd enjoyed the graffiti but he wasn't happy about some of the places they were doing it but he really felt that, at this point, he had no choice.

Flag: Why would Josh feel he couldn't tell the others how he really felt? What do you think about this? Have you ever just gone along with something your friends or family wanted to do even though you weren't really happy about it? Are there times when this would be OK? When wouldn't it be OK?

It was the Friday morning of the first week when things really went wrong. They were working on a wall out the back of St. Peter's Square, next to the adventure playground. Josh was in the middle of his most elaborate project to date and was really concentrating on outlining the final part. Nabil stood and watched admiringly.

'That's brilliant,' he said quietly. It was about 5.30am and although it was light, there was absolutely no-one about. Amar was supposed to be keeping a look out but as usual he decided to take out his computer game. He was so busy playing that he didn't notice the curtains move to the side in the house opposite.

Mrs Travis looked out of the window. She took a sharp intake of breath.

'Now I've got you,' she thought. She had recognised Josh straight away.

He had been in the Youth Club she'd run last year. She didn't recognise the other two boys but she was pretty sure she could describe them to the police.

'I'll put a stop to this once and for all,' she thought. She was absolutely fed up of seeing the neighbourhood scarred by these thugs. She went straight to the phone and dialled the local station.

Flag: Why did Mrs Travis call the boys 'thugs'? What do you think of this? How would you describe them? Do you think Josh had made a good choice here? What else could he have done?

Ten minutes later, a police car screeched to a stop directly next to the wall. Two police officers got out of the car and approached the boys. Josh had just turned as he heard the brakes but Nabil and Amar had seen the car coming. They didn't stop. They simply ran and left Josh to face the two police officers on his own. He had no choice but to stay put. He couldn't run. He was surrounded.

Ending point: At this point, the following two endings can be read to the students. The facilitator can then ask the students to judge which is the better ending, that is, which one would achieve the best possible outcome for those involved. The students can then be asked to work out the best ending for themselves via the first Circle Time activity listed in the Activities section.

Ending one

Josh put his head down. He knew there was no way out of this one. The first officer turned to him and said, 'Well, we've caught you red–handed. No good denying it. You'd better come down to the Station with us.'

They opened the car door and he got in the back with the second officer. 'We'll have to contact your parents,' he said 'so you'd better give us their number.'

Josh nodded. He couldn't speak. He just felt awful. He knew his mum would go totally bananas and she'd never let Nabil and Amar come and stay again. That's when he made up his mind – he'd say he didn't know the other two. He'd say they just happened to come along and watch him but that they weren't from round here and he'd never seen them before. He thought about this as the car made its way to the station. When they got there he was met by someone from the Youth Offending Team who said she'd be with him throughout the interview.

Fifty minutes later, Josh had stuck to his story. The police officer's said they wanted to take a break from the interview so they all moved out to the main foyer where they were given cups of tea and coffee.

Josh took on sip of his tea and breathed a sigh of relief. I think they believed me and at least it will only be me in trouble now, he thought, not seeing his mum walk past the side entrance. She looked furious. Her face was purple as were those of Nabil and Amar whom she dragged along beside her.

Ending two

Josh didn't know where to look. He was amazed that they'd been spotted and absolutely furious that Nabil and Amar had run off.

It was their idea anyway in the first place, he thought. How could they just dump me in it like this. It's not fair. It's just not fair.

He then had a brainwave. The can of paint had rolled into the gutter. It was behind the two police officers. They obviously hadn't seen it.

'Well, I think you've got some explaining to do son,' said the older policeman.

'I know it looks weird – but honestly, this wasn't me. I was just walking round, looking at it. I'm on my way to my paper round. That's why I'm up so early. The two boys that ran off, they were doing the graffiti. I stood and watched them for a bit that's all, honest.'

The two policemen looked at each other. Then the younger one said,

'I have to admit, I don't recognise you. We do know most of the kids round here that do this stuff. We've got a lot of them on CCTV and there are nearly always eye witnesses. Your face is definitely not familiar.'

Josh breathed a sigh of relief.

'Still, we'll need to take your details and for you to come down to the Station to give a description of the other kids. You didn't know them, did you?'

'No,' said Josh. 'I don't think they're from round here.'

He got into the police car. He didn't notice Mrs Travis open her front door to look as the car went past. But then again, he wouldn't, would he?

Activities

Use Circle Time as a vehicle to problem-solve. Discuss the two endings and ask the students which they prefer and why? Do they think Josh made a good choice? Which choice would they have made? What do they think he should do next? What advice would they give him?

Students can formulate a definition(s) for 'anti-social behaviour.' What would they include in this definition and why?

Set up a debate focusing on the question: Why is it important to look after our environment? Students can role-play similar scenes and act out a 'better ending' to the story, that is, one in which Josh makes a better choice.

Work outside school

Students can develop a questionnaire in order to find out what others do in order to keep their community safe and places to live, healthy. They can interview a range of different people including local police officers, park warden, environmental health team members and refuse collectors.

Reflection

Students can reflect on their own experiences. Have they ever participated in an activity that they knew to be wrong? Did they think of the consequences? Did they consider the options?

Why is it so difficult to always stick up for your own beliefs? Is it so important to be able to do this? Can we choose our behaviours or will we naturally be influenced by others? If you lie, do you always get found out? Has this happened to you? If so, did it make you think more carefully about lying in the future?

Session 8: Losing Gran

Focus

▸ awareness that loss and grief affects all of us at some point in our lives

▸ understanding how loss and bereavement can change behaviour

▸ understanding how self-reflection can help us to cope more effectively with difficult situations

▸ recognising when we need to elicit help and support to cope with overpowering emotions.

This story is about a girl who is suffering from the loss of her grandmother. They had developed a very strong relationship and spent a great deal of time together, mainly due to the fact that both of her parents worked full-time and she had consequently been looked after by her grandmother. Unfortunately her grandmother had been diagnosed with stomach cancer nine months earlier and although she had been very sick for the last three weeks prior to her death, no-one in the family had fully explained to Melissa what was actually going to happen, that is, the fact that this was terminal. The loss and grief subsequently led to some uncharacteristically aggressive behaviours. Melissa has to self-reflect upon her reactions and responses and make the choice about whether or not to seek help.

Either stop the story and discuss the Flag points as you read or read the whole story and use these as discussion points prior to completing the activities.

Melissa walked out of the hospital with her mum and dad. No-one spoke, there was just the awful silence of an ending in the air. There was no more to say. They got into the car and went back to the flat. It was freezing cold so her mum immediately switched on the central heating and went into the kitchen to make a cup of tea. Melissa sat down on the sofa and stared straight ahead – not looking, not thinking and not feeling. She was simply blank like a piece of paper no-one wanted to write on. It was 4.30 in the morning and they had been at the hospital for 14 hours exactly. She had sat by her gran's bed from the moment she'd arrived until the moment her gran had finally died. The phone call to school had been made at about 2.30pm. Melissa had been called up to Mrs Bartlett's, the head teacher office. She had been kind. She'd made her a cup of tea and then said, 'Please sit down. Have a sip of tea, Melissa. Now, I've got to tell you some very difficult news. I'm afraid your mum has just phoned from the hospital. Apparently, your gran has told her that she thinks she's going now.'

'Going, going where? She can't go anywhere, she can't get out of bed at the moment!' said Melissa in astonishment.

Mrs Bartlett took hold of her hand and held it for what seemed like an age.

'I'm afraid, um, she means your gran thinks that she's dying and they want you to go up to the hospital straight away.'

'But she can't be dying, she would have told me and she said only yesterday she wanted to get better for my birthday party next week,' said Melissa, almost shouting at the head teacher. She didn't feel like crying. She just felt shocked and angry.

'I'm going to drive you there myself, OK? I'll just pop out and get my coat then we'll get away,' said Mrs Bartlett. She could see Melissa was distressed and she wanted to get her up and out as soon as she could.

> **Flag:** Have you ever had a shock like this that left you feeling numb? Why do you think her gran may not have told her she was dying? Why would this make Melissa feel angry, or would it? How do you think most people would feel if they were about to lose someone that they loved very much?

Once they had arrived at the hospital, Melissa couldn't believe what she saw. The day before, her gran had been sitting up in bed, talking about what she would wear to Melissa's birthday party. She now lay back on the pillows and her eyes were closed. She looked very pale and very fragile. She had three drips around her bed and it was obvious to Melissa that she had been pumped full of morphine. But she still didn't look comfortable. There was a frown mark between her eyes and she was dribbling slightly from her half open mouth.

Melissa got a tissue from the box at the side of the bed and wiped her gran's mouth. She knew that she'd hate for anyone to see her like that. She was always so particular about how she looked and about being clean and smart. She always said, 'You may not have money but you can always have clean clothes, hair and shoes!' She must have been the only patient on the ward who insisted that her hair was combed through every day and that she put on her lipstick and powder – no matter how bad she felt. As Melissa cleaned the side of her face she woke up and looked directly at her.

'Hello love,' she said.

'Hello Gran,' said Melissa.

'You are a darling, you know. I don't think you'll ever know how much I love you. No, not ever.'

And that was it – the last thing she said to Melissa. The last thing she said to anyone. After that there were six hours of soiling the bed, sweats and wailing followed by the last few hours when her gran simply seemed to drift off into unconsciousness. It wasn't possible to see if she was aware of anyone or anything. She just breathed more and more lightly until her head rolled back and she let out one last sigh. Then there was silence apart from Melissa's mum who lay across her gran's shoulder crying.

'Oh Mum, Mum …I'm so sorry, Mum.'

 Flag: How do you think Melissa felt when she saw the change in her gran? Have you ever lost anyone special and precious? Did anything help? Or anyone?

It was two weeks before Melissa went back to school. The first day was the hardest of all as she just felt so down that she still didn't want to get out of bed. The problem was also, however, that she felt really, really angry. She felt angry with her mum and dad because they didn't seem to want to talk about her gran. It was almost as if her gran hadn't lived or been a part of their lives at all. Her mum and dad almost seemed to have shut out all those memories of her. Melissa also felt very angry with her gran and this was probably the hardest bit to deal with.

'Why hadn't she told me? Why didn't she say anything to me? Why did she lie to me?' were the questions that kept running through her mind.

 Flag: Why do you think Melissa's mum and dad seemed to be acting in this way? What do you think the atmosphere would have been like at home? Was Melissa 'right' to feel angry with her gran as well? Do you think these feelings are normal or natural when such things happen to you? What are your views and experiences?

Melissa spent the first part of the morning feeling extremely tense, trying to avoid all the pitying glances from her friends and the teachers. She didn't want them to feel sorry for her. She just wanted them to go away and leave her alone. There was only one friend who seemed to make her feel less tense. Carl came and sat by her in the art lesson. He didn't say anything. He just sat next to her and did his work. He passed the pens and paints next. He didn't say, 'Oh I'm so sorry about your gran. You must be feeling horrible.' He was just there.

Flag: Is wanting to be 'on your own' something you've experienced? Why do you think we need this sometimes? What do you think of Carl's behaviours? How did he seem to know what was the 'right' thing to do when other students and the teachers didn't seem to?

After the art lesson, the class went out to play and that's when things seemed to get worse for Melissa. She didn't feel like joining in with anything so she simply sat down on the bench at the side of the football pitch. She watched the others in silence. She felt completely blank and that she somehow wasn't quite there in that place at all. It was like she was standing up on some kind of platform, overlooking or looking in at what they were all doing – like an outsider or a being from another planet. It was odd but she felt that in a funny way, she could cope with feeling like this. Unfortunately, this feeling didn't last as within a few minutes she was surrounded by a group of girls. They'd all come over to see how she was and to see if there was anything she needed or wanted. They wanted to help.

'Oh, we're so sorry Melissa,' said Amy.

'Yes,' said Teresa, 'we just heard the news and we knew you'd be feeling awful. Do you want me to get you a drink?'

'Or do you want some of my crisps?'

'Do you want me to sit with you?'

'Shall I ask if we can go to the Quiet Room?'

'You can just cry on me if you like, I don't mind.'

The last comment was the one that hit the fuse. Melissa just saw red. She stood up and pushed through the group of girls, hitting out at them as she went.

'No, no I don't. Just go away and leave me alone. You're just nosy cows, I don't want you anywhere near me!'

The girls stood back in amazement and watched as Melissa ran across the playground and into the main school building.

'That's not Melissa,' said Amy rubbing her arm where she'd been hit.

'No, I've never seen her hit anyone before,' said Teresa.

They stared after her wondering what to do next.

Flag: Why would feeling as if you weren't really 'in' a situation actually help? Have you ever experienced this sensation? How would Melissa be feeling when the girls were questioning her? Are you surprised she reacted in this way?

Ending point: At this point, the following two endings can be read to the students. The facilitator can then ask the students to judge which is the better ending, that is, which one would achieve the best possible outcome for those involved. The students can then be asked to work out the best ending for themselves via the first Circle Time activity listed in the Activities section.

Ending one

Melissa ran to the toilets. She ran into the first cubicle, slammed the door, shut and locked it. She sat down and put her head in her hands. She sobbed. It was like an explosion. All her anger and grief seemed to stream out. This went on for at least twenty minutes but she was oblivious to this fact. Time was of no importance. When she'd finally stopped she sat up and wiped her eyes. She heard a faint knock at the door then a quiet voice said, 'Melissa – is that you?'

It was Mrs Samuels. She'd been on duty in the playground and had seen what had happened and decided to see if she was alright. Melissa bit her lip. She liked Mrs Samuels but she didn't want to talk. She just wanted to be on her own. She said nothing.

'Look… um… I know you probably don't want to talk but I just want you to know that I'm here for you. I lost my mum in the summer and she died of cancer like your gran so I really do know how you feel. If you want to you can come to my office and have a talk. It might help.'

'What's the point?' said Melissa quietly.

Mrs. Samuels looked taken aback. She wasn't quite sure how to respond to that.

'Well sometimes it can help to talk but I am here if you need me,' she said.

'Yeah, well, I'd rather stay here. I don't think I need your sort of help,' said Melissa as she opened the cubicle door. She looked angry. It was as if the offer of help had been a slap in the face. She walked straight past Mrs Samuels and back out into the playground.

Ending two

Melissa kicked the toilet door repeatedly. She was crying at the same time. It was as if she simply didn't know how to let out her anger any other way other than hitting out. As she kicked she could see the group of girls surrounding her. She wanted them all to die – just like her gran had done. They deserved it. Her gran didn't.

She sat down on the floor exhausted. She put her head down into her hands and held it in almost as if to stop it from exploding. Then she heard someone walk in. When she looked up she saw Carl. He crept over to her looking around nervously.

'Look I'm a boy as you know. I'm not supposed to be here. If I get caught I'll never live it down. They'll start calling me Carla,' he said.

Melissa looked at him. He looked so embarrassed and uncomfortable, almost in pain. She couldn't help it. All of a sudden she started to laugh. She was laughing and crying at the same time.

'Come on, quick. Get out of here before I'm found out,' he said. He held out his hand. Melissa took it and followed him out of the girl's toilets.

Once they were outside he gave her a tissue. 'Look, I know you just want to be left alone so I'm not going to talk or anything or ask you to talk. I'll just stay with you in lessons if you want.'

'OK,' she said.

'But you know Mrs Samuel's mum died don't you? I think it might help to talk to her when you feel you can. Will you do that?' he asked.

Melissa smiled weakly 'I might do. I'll think about it,' she said as they both walked off to the next lesson.

Activities

Use Circle Time as a vehicle to problem-solve. What do you think would have been the best ending to this story? Would it have been an ending or a beginning? What would really have helped Melissa when she went back to school? What could have been done by the other students and the staff?

How do people remember loved ones who have died? Ask the students to brainstorm this question and to present a joint display of ideas, rites and rituals such as special services, memory books, photograph albums, thinking time and memorials.

Discuss the grief cycle and its different stages. Ask the students to suggest how individuals might think, feel and act at each stage of this process.

Melissa chose not to talk to Mrs Samuels in the first ending. Why might talking be helpful? Students can brainstorm this question and also investigate the kinds of support systems which would be available to students in their school who may be suffering a bereavement or significant loss or change.

Work outside school

Ask the students to investigate how different cultures and religions mark and celebrate death. What do they believe? What are their views on the so called after life? What are the customs and rituals surrounding the funeral? What is expected of the bereaved family?

They can gather information from a variety of written resources alongside interviewing members of their own family, community and religious leaders. It may be useful for students to work in groups on this activity to present the facts in an information sheet to share with the group as a whole at a later stage. It may be useful to place students in mixed faith groups and to nominate each group to a particular faith system.

Reflection

Ask the students to put themselves in Melissa's shoes. How do they think they would behave? What feelings would they have at this time? Would they have similar thoughts, feelings and behaviours to Melissa? If so, why? If not, why not? Why is it so hard to lose a loved one? Are there people you feel you can talk to about times when you experience overpowering emotions? Who? Why?

Why do we need to build such relationships? What might happen if we don't have such people or we choose not to communicate our stresses, anger or guilt?

Session 9: The Split

Focus

▶ awareness that change can often be a difficult or painful process

▶ consideration of others feelings and empathy

▶ understanding that relationships may not be permanent

▶ understanding that relationships can survive and be maintained if those involved both feel the same way

▶ attempting to manipulate others or control them by our own behaviours may not achieve the best possible outcome.

This story is about a boy whose parents have recently split up. He finds it extremely difficult to accept the fact that they no longer want to be together and also feels that, to some extent, he may have been the cause of their break-up. A further complication is added when his mum meets a new partner and asks him to move into their family home. Jamal finds this an intolerable situation and becomes determined to cause a rift between the two in the hope that his mum and dad will get back together again. When he realises that his plan has not worked he then has to make the choice as to whether or not to change his attitude and behaviours.

Either stop the story and discuss the Flag points as you read or read the whole story and use these as discussion points prior to completing the activities.

Jamal was looking forward to seeing his dad at the weekend. It felt like ages since they last spent any time together. In fact, it was only seven days but it felt like seven years to him. He missed his dad so much and wished that things had been different. Unfortunately they weren't. This was reality. They had finally split up and, according to his dad, that was the end of it all. They had tried to make a go of it. Both his parents had said this again and again. But they just couldn't keep to the rules. They argued non-stop and it was always about the same old things, namely the housework, money and Jamal himself. His mum was continually saying how soft his dad was on him.

'He let's you get away with murder,' she often said. Jamal didn't think that was true. He though his dad was kind and he just liked to have a laugh and muck about. They did loads of stuff together like football, basketball and playing computer games. They just seemed to like the same things but again that annoyed his mum.

'I can understand Jamal playing those games,' she'd say, 'after all he is 11 years old, but I don't get it with Vernon. I mean, he's supposed to be an adult!' It was at times like that that he hated his mum. She was just too good at the put-downs.

> **Flag:** What do you think 'keeping to the rules' in a relationship means? Do you have rules in your relationships? Are these different for each one? For example, with friends, parents/carers and teachers. How do you think Jamal's dad would feel about this sort of put-down? Why do we use 'put-downs'? What purpose do you think they serve?

But then, his dad also seemed to be able to use equally as abrasive put-downs to his mum. It was like they were in a competition to see who could hurt each other the most. Then in the middle of all of this was Jamal, who sometimes felt like he was a goal-keeper, ducking and diving and trying to catch their insults before they actually got to each other and did some real damage. There were other times though when he felt like the ball being kicked around the pitch.

His mum would tell his dad how she'd had a phone call from the teacher at school to say Jamal had been playing up again and that if this inappropriate behaviour continued they would have to think about excluding him for a few days. Then his dad would say, 'Those teachers don't know what they're talking about. They're only picking on him because he's a black kid.' Then his mum would start shouting, saying it was no use going on about race and that the only reason Jamal was in trouble was because his dad had spoilt him. She'd say, 'You've let him get away with blue murder. You've given him no boundaries whatsoever. He's spoilt and won't take no for an answer. You've not given him any boundaries. It's your fault.' That's when Jamal would get angry – not just because of what she'd said but because he felt that they were arguing about him. It was his fault. He was to blame. And now he thought that he was to blame for their split, especially because he had then been excluded from school – not just once, but three times so far.

Flag: Do you think teachers 'choose' to pick on certain students? Do you think it's the student or the student's behaviour that is the issue? Have you ever felt that your boundaries weren't clear? What did this feel like? What happened?

Anyway, things seemed to have calmed down a little just lately – mainly because Jamal was able to see his dad more regularly. It had become quite difficult during and just after the time his dad had moved out as he'd had to find himself a bed-sit and then sort out some new furniture and kitchen things. It was a while before he'd settled and managed to buy a pull-down foam bed so that Jamal could comfortably stay overnight. He'd also had to ask permission from his new landlady for Jamal to stay. She'd said it was fine as long as he was well behaved, flushed the toilet properly and didn't bring any pets. The latter wasn't a problem as he'd never had a pet anyway.

Flag: How do you think Jamal's dad felt about leaving their home? How easy is it to make a new start like this? How would you feel if you had to move away and start afresh in a new school?

Eventually, the time came for his dad to pick him up. Jamal was excited and nervous at the same time. His mum seemed oddly nervous too. Just before his dad drove up, she turned to him and said,

'Look, I need to tell you something. Your dad knows about it so you can talk to him. You know I've been out with Stephen a few times don't you? The man I met at the club. You got on well with him when he came round to play cards the other week. Well, we've been seeing each other for a couple of months and … well, we really get on well. So, he's going to move in this weekend while you're at your dad's. I know this will come as a bit of a surprise but I do want you to feel OK about it. You will won't you? For my sake?'

Jamal stared at her. He didn't know what to say. He just felt numb. Then he heard the car drive up. He turned to walk out. He didn't say goodbye to his mum or give her a kiss as he'd usually do. He just looked directly at her as if he couldn't believe what she'd just said. Then he left the house.

Flag: What do you think of Jamal's response? How does he feel? How would you think, feel and behave if you were in his shoes? How does his mum feel? Do people have the 'right' to have good relationships or are they just lucky if they manage to achieve this?

From that moment on, it was war. As soon as Stephen moved in, Jamal knew he was going to hate him. It wasn't that he was horrible or unkind. He really tried to get on with Jamal and to talk to him about things. But, he was just the absolute opposite of his dad and Jamal missed his dad so much. Stephen hated sports and computers. He liked collecting stamps and listening to music. Jamal could think of nothing more boring. They had absolutely nothing in common. Worst of all, he believed in rules. Everything was rules, rules, rules. As soon as he walked in he started laying down the law about every aspect of their home life.

'You really should have a rule about sitting at the table for the evening meal,' he'd say. Jamal couldn't see why sitting with a tray on your lap in front of the TV was so bad.

But worst of all were the rules he suddenly made up for Jamal and the way in which his mum went along with it all. There were so many of them: he now had to get up at 7.00 am sharp, he had to use the bathroom between 7.10 am and 7.20 am, he had to pack his bag for school the night before, he had to do his homework and have it checked by Stephen every night before he was allowed thirty minutes on the computer. He had to lose his computer time if the work wasn't considered good enough and he had to go to bed at 9.00 pm before any of the good programmes came on TV. He was so fed up. He'd never had so many rules in his life. Stephen kept saying it was just so that Jamal could get on better at school and so that things in the house could run more smoothly. His mum was delighted.

Flag: Is the parent-child relationship special? If so, why?

Why do you think Jamal would find these rules difficult? What would happen if there were no rules at home? What are your rules and do they help or make things more stressful?

Jamal couldn't bear it. He moaned, he shouted and he swore. Then he gave up and just went along with it. At least he did on the surface. Underneath he was desperately thinking how he could manage to get rid of Stephen. He wanted him out of their house. Most of all he wanted his dad back and their comfortable, relaxed life-style to continue. Then he had an idea.

That night, when he got back from school, he went up to his mum's bedroom (only now it was his mum's and Stephen's but he didn't like to think about that). He went over to the chest of drawers by the window. He opened the top drawer and pulled out two savings tins – one marked Mum and one marked

Jamal. They were what his mum called their holiday tins. She put £5 a week in each tin so by the time they went to Barbados at Christmas they both had loads of spending money. Jamal loved counting it all up and thinking about all the treats he'd be able to buy for himself and his cousins when he got out there. He took out all the notes from each tin. He carefully piled them together and then went to the wardrobe where he placed them in the inside pocket of Stephen's leather jacket. The one thing he knew his mum hated more than anything was a thief. 'This has got to work,' he thought.

He waited until they both got in from work and then mentioned to his mum that they hadn't counted their holiday money since his dad left. Could they do it tonight? His mum was pleased that for once he seemed to be a little more positive and she agreed. However, her pleasure turned to shock once she found the money was gone and she was horrified when Jamal then said, 'I think I saw Stephen in your drawer the other day, Mum. Do you think he might have taken it because he needed a loan?' His mum flinched. She looked uneasy. Stephen looked horrified.

'The one thing I'm not is a thief,' he said. 'Just check in my jackets – go on. I'm not having this.' He glared at Jamal who smiled back at him. His mum went upstairs. When she came down she was holding the bundle of notes in her hand. She was red in the face and near to tears. 'Get out!' she shouted. 'I can't believe you did this! Get out!'

Flag: What do you think of Jamal's behaviour? Was he right to set-up Stephen? Has he thought about how his mum will feel now or how she might feel if she found out the truth?

Ending point: At this point, the following two endings can be read to the students. The facilitator can then ask the students to judge which is the better ending, that is, which one would achieve the best possible outcome for those involved. The students can then be asked to work out the best ending for themselves via the first Circle Time activity listed in the Activities section.

Ending one

Jamal's mum cried and cried. It went on for days. It seemed like she just couldn't cope with it. Jamal began to feel really bad. He hadn't liked Stephen but he hadn't realised just how much his mum had liked him. Every night he'd come home from school and find her in tears. She'd been signed off work for the last week. She'd gone to the doctors and he'd given her some tablets to try and help her get over it. Stephen phoned almost every day. He wanted to explain that he wasn't a thief, that he hadn't done it. He knew that it was Jamal but he didn't say that. Jamal was confused about that.

Anyway, he went over to his dad's that weekend but didn't really enjoy it. He was too worried about his mum. When he got back she was sitting on the sofa in her dressing gown.

'I just felt too fed up to get dressed,' she said. 'I really loved Stephen you know. I still do. I just can't believe he did it.' She started to cry. Then Jamal made up his mind. He had to tell. It wasn't going to be easy but he had to do it.

Ending two

Jamal was delighted. He felt worry for his mum but he knew she'd be alright in a few days. She was tough like him. But when he found her crying a few days later he realised he'd been wrong. He got on the phone to his dad and asked him to come over. Maybe they'd make up. Maybe his mum would be glad to see him and want him again instead of the thief Stephen.

It didn't quite work out like that. His dad was his usual nice self. He said how sorry he was but then said he'd have to go as his new girlfriend Carla was waiting in the car.

'Oh,' said his mum, 'Where did you meet her?'

'At work,' he said. 'I've known her since she started as a junior about ten years ago. I hadn't realised she'd fancied me for much of that time,' he joked. His mum smiled lamely.

'Good luck,' she said.

Jamal couldn't believe it. He ran upstairs. He didn't say goodbye to his dad. He was too angry. He sat down on his bed and punched the pillow. Then he stopped. He'd made up his mind. It had worked with his mum and Stephen. Why shouldn't it work with his dad and Carla?

Activities

Use Circle Time as a vehicle to problem-solve. What do they think would have been a better ending to this story? What could Jamal have done in order to have had a better outcome for both his parents and himself? What needed to change for these characters? How could Jamal cope more effectively with the changes at home?

The students can debate the question, 'Is it ever right to lie in order to get what you want?'

Work outside school

Students can investigate the effects of divorce and separation. What are the statistics? What are the outcomes? Are there benefits for some and what are these? They can present 'Fact Finding' sheets which may then engender further discussion.

Reflection

Ask the students to put themselves in Jamal's shoes. How would they feel? What would they think and do? Can they see a way forward? How do they cope with change?

Why is it important to be able to do this? What kinds of changes are most difficult for them? What coping strategies do they currently have? What one do they need to develop?

Session 10: The Cheat

Focus

▶ awareness of stress and how it affects us physically and emotionally

▶ understanding the importance of valuing ourselves and our right to be who we are

▶ using brain and feelings to inform behaviour

▶ understanding the need to think about the consequences of our behaviours

▶ saying how we feel about others perceptions of us and challenging misconceptions and labelling.

This story is about a girl who makes the choice to cheat in her KS2 SATs examinations. The students have been gearing up for the tests for the whole of the previous term and many of them have begun to feel quite pressurised and stressed. It has been emphasised to them (wrongly) that their results will determine the secondary schools that they will attend in the next academic year. Those who do particularly well are more likely to gain a place at the more popular and 'academic' high school. The children all believe this. Kelly is not considered a particularly high achiever but most of her friends are. She makes the decision to cheat in her English paper so that she can gain a higher score and then hopefully go to the same school as her friends.

Either stop the story and discuss the Flag points as you read or read the whole story and use these as discussion points prior to completing the activities.

Kelly opened her eyes and stared up at the ceiling. She watched the mobile turn slowly in the gentle breeze coming from the open window. It was already hot and she could feel a drop of sweat on her forehead which she wiped away with her hand. Her mum had said yesterday that it was a 'freak' summer because it shouldn't ever be quite so hot in May. She put it down to global warming. She moaned about this problem incessantly. It had almost become an obsession with her but Kelly liked to listen to her sound off. Her mum always sounded so clever and everyone listened to what she had to say. 'I wish I was like her,' she thought secretly to herself but feeling and fearing that this would never be the case.

'I'll never be like Mum. I'm just too thick and it's all too hard for me,' she thought. 'Even Mum knows that.'

She thought about last night and how her mum had tried to help her with her spellings. Kelly continually got most of them wrong and was near to tears by the end of the list. Her mum had given her a hug and said, 'At least you're a tryer – I'll give you that Kelly.' But Kelly didn't want to be a tryer, she just wanted to be the same as her friends who could easily have got them all right.

Flag: Is it a good thing to be 'clever'? What do we mean by this? Are there different ways of being clever? How do you think Kelly feels about her mum's comment? Is she being labelled? Is this fair, just or helpful?

Kelly made herself get out of bed and get into the shower. Her whole body ached. It was almost as if she had flu; she just felt so tired and weak.

Spelling

Well today's the day, she thought. It was the first of their SATS tests and she wasn't looking forward to it at all. In fact, she felt physically sick at the thought of even setting foot in the school, let alone the classroom that had been set up specifically for this purpose. She had felt sick every day for the last six weeks. It was almost as if someone had tied an enormous knot in her stomach and been pulling it tighter and tighter as each day progressed. Today it seemed to be tighter than ever before, as if it was just about to burst open through her stomach and splatter its contents all over the bathroom.

Flag: Kelly could be described as being stressed. Do you agree? What is stress? Who gets it? Is it the same for everybody? Which are the worst and least worst forms and causes of stress? Do you think the stressors that children have are less important or significant than those that adults experience?

Once she'd showered and dressed, Kelly went downstairs. Her mum was humming a tune to herself while frying some eggs. Kelly looked at her and wandered if she knew how scared she felt.

I mustn't show it, she thought. 'Mum will just think I'm a wimp.'

Her mum turned round and smiled at her.

'Do you want a fried egg sandwich?' she asked. 'I know we don't normally do this but I thought it might be a good idea to have something a bit more substantial before you first test.'

'Thanks Mum,' Kelly said not wanting to eat anything. The thought of food made her physically wince but she made herself gulp down the runny egg and bread, which then sat like a big lump on top of the knot in her tummy. They cleared up and then went out to the car. Her mum put on the radio and started to sing along.

They didn't talk until they reached the school gates when her mum leaned over, gave her a hug, and said, 'Don't worry. It's only a little test. It's not that important. You just do your best, that's all you can do darling?'

Kelly got out of the car. She wanted to scream at her mum, 'But my best isn't good enough!' But she didn't. She walked into the playground and joined her friends who had congregated in an over-excited huddle near the adventure area.

Flag: Do you think Kelly should have told her mum about how stressed she was feeling? Would this have been a good choice? Why? Was it helpful for her mum to say it was just a 'little test?' Do adults sometimes suggest or think that children's stressors are not that important? Have you experienced this? What could be done to change this perception? What would you do?

Kelly looked at her friends. Emma, Charlie and Nisha were laughing and joking with each other. It was almost as if they were excited about the test. Kelly couldn't understand it. 'Why would anyone get excited by it?' she thought. Then she suddenly realised that it was probably because for all of them, this would be a walkover. They were all dead clever. They knew all the answers and they would get everything right. None of them would have a problem. She stood by the side of the group, almost like an outsider looking in.

'God, my dad made me go through those spellings three times last night,' said Emma. 'He was just determined I'd get every one of them right and I did you know.'

'Well, they're not that difficult,' said Charlie. 'My mum says it's all about self-belief anyway. She says if you think you can learn something then you will. It will just come automatically.'

'Not if you're thick like me it won't,' said Kelly, almost surprising herself at the angry tone in her voice.

'Oh don't say that,' said Emma. 'You're not thick.'

'Well, why is it so hard for me then and not for you lot? It's not fair.'

She walked away from them in the direction of the classrooms. Emma went to go after her but Charlie pulled her back.

'Don't,' he said. 'She needs to be on her own for a bit, she's just in a state.'

'She's been like that for ages,' said Nisha. 'I think it's the worry about next year. I just wish there was something we could do. I don't want her to go to Aylands. I want her to come to Highfield with us but she won't if she doesn't make the grade.'

'It's a shame she's not good at her work,' said Charlie as they followed Kelly into the school building.

Flag: Is it fair that some people find work easier than others? Does it make them 'better' people? Is it possible for everyone to be the same and have the same level of skills? What would happen if this were the case?

Ten minutes later, all of them were sitting at their desks, the test papers placed upside down in front of them. Mr Matthews smiled and wished them all good luck before uttering the words that Kelly had dreaded hearing for the last term and a half. 'You may begin.'

She turned over the test paper. At first it was like she couldn't see it. Her heart was beating so fast and her head was pounding. It seemed that the letters on the page were jumping about all over the place. She looked next to her and saw Emma writing already. She took a deep breath and closed her eyes. She looked back at the page and realised that she could actually answer the first two questions. She picked up her pen and began to fill in the missing words. Then she came to question three and realised that she just didn't get it. She didn't understand it. She didn't have a clue. She could feel her heart begin to pound. Then she looked to her right. She could see Nisha's paper. She was left handed and always pulled her work to the edge of the table and worked at a slant so as to avoid smudging her work. Kelly could see every word. She didn't stop to think about what she was doing. She felt she just had to do it. She copied everything that Nisha wrote.

'I might not be clever,' she thought, 'but I'm a quick writer.'

She didn't think about what might happen if she got caught. It wasn't important. What was important was to get that higher grade and get to Highfield High. Nothing else mattered.

Flag: If you are nervous or stressed what can you do to help yourself? What advice could you give to Kelly? What do you think about her behaviour? Is this a wise choice? Has she really used her brain and her feelings to inform her behaviours? What might the consequences be?

Ending point: At this point, the following two endings can be read to the students. The facilitator can then ask the students to judge which is the better ending, that is, which one would achieve the best possible outcome for those involved. The students can then be asked to work out the best ending for themselves via the first Circle Time activity listed in the Activities section.

Ending one

Just as Nisha turned over her page, Kelly moved her chair slightly nearer so that she could see the answers more easily, then she suddenly went cold. Standing directly behind her was Mr Matthews. She froze. Had he seen? He walked around the back of her row and then moved to the front of the room. Kelly watched him carefully. He sat down at his desk, leant back in his chair and yawned.

Phew, she thought. He hasn't seen me. She turned around to look at Nisha's paper and then took a sharp intake of breath. Nisha had moved her paper. It was too far away. Kelly couldn't see the answers any more. Oh please, please – move it back, she thought. But it was no good. Nisha didn't move. Kelly felt sick. She looked at the paper and then looked up at the clock. There was ten minutes to go before their time was up.

She felt the tears prick her eyes.

It's no good – this won't get me enough marks. I might as well give up now. She screwed up her test paper, stood up and ran from the room.

Ending two

Kelly wrote the answers as fast as she could. Her writing was a mess. She knew it was but that's what happened when you wrote too fast. She got to the end of the second page and then suddenly stopped. It was as if she'd just realised what she was doing. Her brain had suddenly started working.

It's no good, she thought as she put down her pen. What's the point? If I cheat and get good marks, I'll end up in a school where all the other kids are clever. I won't cope with it all.

She stared at her sheet and suddenly the anger and stress seemed to drain away. She began to cry. She cried silently, huge tears rolling down her face and falling on to the page in front of her.

Mr Matthews walked over to her and asked if she wanted to go outside for a moment. She nodded unable to speak. As they got to the door he said, 'Do you want to tell me something?' He said it in the way that makes you feel everything's not quite so bad.

'Yes please,' said Kelly wiping her face. 'I think it would be the best thing to do now.'

Activities

Use Circle Time as a vehicle to problem-solve. Which of the endings is going to get the best outcome for Kelly? What would they like to see happen? What ending would they create? What needs to happen now? Who can help Kelly and how? How can she help herself?

Students can brainstorm identifying all the different ways in which people might cheat such as in a board or card game, in a test, in football or another physical game or in getting someone to take your driving test. These can be written on to small cards. Students can then work in smaller groups in order to place these cards in order of significance: Which is the most serious form of cheating and which is the least serious? Which would have the most negative and least negative impact on the person cheating and on those around him? Students can feed back to the group as a whole giving reasons for their rankings.

Students can consider the best and most healthy ways to cope with stress. They can identify the most common stressors that they may have experienced and then identify the ways in which they might cope with these more effectively, such as talking through the problem with a friend, exercise, time out, relaxation, music, TV or watching a DVD. They may wish to collate the information into a Stress Buster Booklet for children.

Work outside school

Ask the students to devise a questionnaire for parents or carers or other adults in the community on the subject of cheating. What do people feel about this? What do they think is the most damaging form of cheating? What do they consider to be the best ways of dealing with people who behave in this way? How would they help the 'cheats' to change their behaviours? The results can be fed back to the group as a whole and similarities and differences identified.

Reflection

Ask the students to put themselves in Kelly's shoes. How would they feel? What would they think and do?

How could they cope more effectively? Have they ever experienced similar feelings? When? Why? How do they feel about being a 'clever' student?

Is it important to them? Should it be?

Do they think every child matters? If not, why not? If so, why? What can they do to show every child matters and what can the adults around them do?

Session II: Breaking the Rules

Focus

▶ using brain and feelings to inform behaviour

▶ distinguishing between aggressive and assertive behaviours

▶ understanding how attacks on self-esteem impact upon feelings and behaviour

▶ thinking ahead to the consequences of behaviour

▶ understanding how rules can support and maintain a safe environment

▶ understanding how rules might be different in different contexts.

This story is about a boy called Jason who continually responds in an aggressive manner to members of his peer group who tease and verbally abuse him. There seems to be a culture of 'fighting back' in his family and he consequently experiences some real difficulties in keeping the rules in school which are quite different from home. He does not understand that it may be possible to stand up for himself in a more assertive way as opposed to hitting out and becoming aggressive. Jason also needs to understand how others wind him up simply because they find it 'funny' or 'a laugh'.

Either stop the story and discuss the Flag points as you read or read the whole story and use these as discussion points prior to completing the activities.

Jason really hated school. He hated everything about it – the work, the teachers and even the other kids. There was really nothing about it that he enjoyed and he couldn't remember going through the school gates and feeling in any way good or happy for at least six months. It had all started when a new boy had started in their class. His name was Carl and he had moved from Coventry with his mum. As soon as he'd walked into the classroom, Jason knew that they just wouldn't get on. He couldn't quite explain it even to himself but there was just something in the look that he gave him that told Jason this was trouble. That look basically said you think you're tough but I'm going to show you. There's only one who can rule around here and that's me. He didn't need to say a word. Jason could just feel it.

> **Flag:** Do you think people can really sense what others are thinking or feeling about them? How could they do this? Could people be mistaken and what problems might this cause?

And unfortunately for him he was right. Carl quickly became very popular. He was considered a good laugh and very easily made friends as the others liked being around him. He was a brilliant footballer and immediately got picked for the team and he was also quick at his work. He just seemed to have it all according to Jason, who quickly began to feel quite jealous of him. However, Carl's one flaw was that many of his jokes were actually directed against those who were a bit weaker or more vulnerable than he was. It wasn't an obvious form of bullying or control but very undermining of others and done in such a way that it didn't often come to the attention of teachers. If it did, then Carl was quite able to shrug it off and say, 'Oh, we were just having a bit of a laugh.'

The problem was that many of the laughs were geared towards Jason. He was an easy target because he just seemed to get very angry very quickly and he was quite prepared to lash out if he got upset, even though he knew it was against the rules to fight.

> **Flag:** Do clever and popular people always keep the rules and act in a responsible way? Should they? If things are easier for us do we have a 'duty' to help and support others? What do we mean by the word 'duty'? Why are some people easier targets for teasing than others? What advice would you give to Jason at this point?

Every day there was something new that Carl found to target. At first, Jason tried to ignore these comments about his shoes, his haircut or his work. The spelling tests were the worst though as Carl's jibes meant that everyone in the class now knew that Jason found it so hard. That's when he found it really difficult to stop reacting. He knew the rules – if you were angry or upset with anyone you were supposed to go and get help or tell them to stop annoying you. They'd practised using assertive 'I' messages a lot during the autumn term. If someone fouled you in football you were supposed to say, 'I don't like that. I want you to stop it now.' Jason had told his dad about it when it was first introduced and he just burst out laughing.

He'd said, 'What a load of old rubbish. Just give them a good kicking, that'll stop them. It's the only way, otherwise they'll walk all over you.' Jason had listened to this and felt slightly uncomfortable.

'But if you get caught, Dad, you get detention because you've broken the rules – you could even get excluded if you kept on acting hard like that.'

'Don't be soft,' his dad had responded. 'You just do it so no-one sees and then they don't mess with you any more. Anyway rules are meant to be broken. Those teachers should get in the real world where real men just have to stick up for themselves. Life isn't a cosy little laugh – the sooner you kids learn that the better.'

Flag: What rules do you have in school? Are they different to the rules at home? Is this the case for most people? What do you think of Jason's dad's response? What does he mean by 'real men'? What do you think of this? What would school life be like for many students if there were no rules about fighting?

Now, however, Jason wasn't so sure that his dad had got it wrong after all. Why shouldn't he just give Carl a good kick? And all the other kids who seemed to find it funny to join in and have a laugh at his expense? What was so wrong about breaking the rules, especially if it meant that he would be able to keep his self-respect? Surely that was more important? Anyway, if he did what his dad had said and didn't get caught it would be fine wouldn't it? Surely that would get him the outcome he wanted – to stop Carl and make sure the other kids knew who was boss now?

Flag: Jason is talking himself through his reasons for breaking the rules. He looks as if he is using his brain and feelings to inform his behaviour choice. Is he? What do you think about this way of thinking? What would you choose to do if you were in his shoes? Do you think you would manage things differently?

The next day he had gone into school determined to stick up for himself and if that meant throwing a few punches then he would just do exactly that. Mr Price had set up a game of rounders for the PE lesson that morning and Carl, Manjit and Lara had been asked to go out into the playground to set up the equipment. Jason watched them as they walked out. He saw Carl nudge Manjit and start to laugh and he was convinced that he'd said something nasty about him. He could feel his fists clenching.

I'm not going to let them get away with it. Not again, not ever, he thought as the rest of the class were called to line up at the door ready for the lesson.

Flag: Were they laughing at Jason? Could he be sure? Do you think he may simply be getting paranoid? Have you ever thought someone was being nasty to you and subsequently found out that you had been wrong about this? How did you feel? What happened?

Mr Price reminded the whole class of the rules. 'Just make sure you all keep them and there should be no problem,' he said. 'Can anyone just recap for us?'

Manjit put up his hand. 'Three bats each, stop at the first base unless it's a good ball and run if it is – and if you get run out go without making a fuss to sit on the outers' bench.'

'Thank you, Manjit,' said Mr Price. 'Right. Let's sort out the teams.' He went along the line allocating A's and B's to each of the students.

'OK, all the A's stand to my right and all the B's to my left. I'm going to toss the coin. If it's heads the A's will bat first and if it's tails the B's will bat first – OK?' he said.

It was tails and the B's let out a big cheer. Everyone always wanted to bat first. Jason was fed up. He was in the A's team and they had to field. He hated fielding as he got bored just running around trying to catch the ball and get the others out. He also hated it when the others started getting rounders because they would boast about it and taunt the opposition. That's exactly what happened this time!

Manjit and Carl were in the B's team and immediately started to laugh as Kevin got the first rounder. Carl turned round to look at Jason who had run like mad in order to try and catch the ball but tripped and missed it just at the last minute. He gave him a sneering smile and said quietly under his breath, 'Better luck next time, loser.'

Carl sneered back at him and felt more determined than ever not to let him get away with it. When it was Carl's turn to bat, Jason was ready. He stood just by the second post. As Carl ran round he put out his foot and tripped him over. He was very careful to make it look like an accident. He'd run after the ball, got near to second base, tripped Carl and then fell over himself to make it look like he couldn't help it.

Flag: Jason had planned his revenge. What do you think of his behaviour? Do you think Carl deserved this? What else could Jason have done in order to cope with Carl's comment? What would you have done?

Carl stood up and rubbed his leg. He was red in the face and obviously really furious. He knew that Jason had tripped him up on purpose.

'I'll get you,' he said under his breath looking over Jason's shoulder to make sure Mr Price wasn't looking.

'Yeah, you and whose army?' replied Jason.

'I don't need an army, I could take you on solo no problem,' said Carl. 'Just name your time and place.'

'After school – tonight – down the park,' said Jason. But unfortunately, he couldn't manage to wait that long. As Carl walked away, he turned round and mouthed the word 'wanker' at Jason. As he did this, Manjit, Charmaine and Kieran saw him and immediately started to laugh out loud looking directly at Jason as they did so. That was it. He just couldn't wait any longer. It was a 'red rag to a bull' as his dad would say. He didn't stop to think or plan. He just went for Carl, running across the field and laying into him – kicking, punching and lashing out repeatedly. He was so taken over by his own anger that he didn't hear the rest of the students shouting, 'Fight, fight, fight.' It was only when he felt someone pulling him away from Carl that he realised his nose was bleeding.

Ending point: At this point, the following two endings can be read to the students. The facilitator can then ask the students to judge which is the better ending, that is, which one would achieve the best possible outcome for those involved. The students can then be asked to work out the best ending for themselves via the first Circle Time activity listed in the Activities section.

Ending one

Ten minutes later, both boys were standing in Miss Steven's office. She looked furious.

'I can't understand this,' she said. 'You both know what the rules are – what on earth did you both think you were doing? You know we don't tolerate fighting in this school. We discuss our problems before they escalate, you should both know that. What on earth caused all of this?' She waved her hand as if to highlight the fact that both boys looked bruised and battered.

Carl looked at Jason. 'He started it,' he said. 'From the moment I walked in this school he's had it in for me – always giving me dirty looks and stuff. I've tried to ignore him but it's been really hard. Then, today, he just went for me – it's like he wanted to really hurt me. I don't know why. I've done nothing to him,' Carl said.

Jason clenched his fists.

'You liar,' he shouted. 'He's lying Miss, it's him. He's been getting at me and getting the others to get at me. It wasn't my fault.'

'But Jason,' interrupted Mrs Stevens. 'You made a choice here. You chose to fight rather than keep to our rules and talk it out. That isn't good. Just think what would happen if we all made that choice. It would be a disaster, there would be utter anarchy in the school – that's why we've got rules and why we need to keep them.'

Jason looked down at the floor. He knew she was right. He knew his dad was wrong but he also knew that Carl was a liar and that he'd make sure he paid for this – big time.

Ending two

Mr Price held both of Jason's arms. 'Now stop – stop and calm down,' he said. His voice didn't sound normal. It was higher and louder than his usual voice. He was obviously shocked by what he had seen. He had always thought that Jason was a bit of a trouble maker but he hadn't quite realised he was capable of so much aggression.

'Now calm down,' he repeated. 'You're going to come with me now Jason and we'll sit down and find out what all this has been about.'

Jason stopped trying to get away from Mr Price. He knew it was useless as he was twice his size and more. He was also a teacher and it was one thing to hit another pupil and quite another if you punched the teacher.

Ten minutes later, they were both sitting back in the classroom. The rest of the class had gone into the hall for an Assembly and Carl had been taken to the Head's office.

Mr Price looked at Jason.

'What got into you?' he asked. 'What is it that made you so angry?'

Jason didn't say anything. What was the point? It wouldn't change things would it?

Mr Price continued. 'You see, even if Carl had started it and you'd just retaliated it would still be bad. You do realise that you will have a fixed term exclusion now, don't you?'

'So,' said Jason, 'I don't care.'

'Oh, but I think that you do care actually,' said Mr. Price. 'You see, I've been watching you over the last few weeks and you seem to have become more and more angry. I know that something's been going on and I know that you're not happy, Jason. Now that can't carry on. I really do hope that we can talk now because I'm sure that you'd prefer to feel happier and good about yourself and I know that's what I'd like.'

'But why, why should how I feel matter to you?' asked Jason in disbelief.

'I promise you, it does matter to me. It's why I do this job – to get kids like you to feel good about themselves. It's more important than anything else I do,' he said.

'So, I'm not sure about it,' said Jason but for the first time in months he actually managed a half smile and it felt so much better.

Activities

Use Circle Time as a vehicle to problem-solve. What would have been the best ending for Jason? Which of the two endings do the students prefer and why? What will get him the best possible outcome? What could he have done differently? Who could have helped him?

Students can make up their own rules for the following: the classroom, the home and the environment. However, they can devise two sets of rules: (a) rules which would get the best outcome and (b) rules which would get the worst outcome. They can work together in smaller groups to devise these and then feedback to the class as a whole.

Students can devise their own games (board games or games for the playground). They can also write the rules and then have time to teach the game to a group of students. It may be helpful to present all the games and sets of rules in a Games Record Book which can be held centrally by the teacher.

Work outside school

Students can scan local and national newspapers in order to identify three or four examples of people who 'broke the rules'. They can consult with parents/carers in order to elicit their views. What do they think of these crimes? Who has it adversely affected? What is the environmental, physical or emotional impact of these behaviours? Do they think that these people made good choices or not? What were the contributory factors? Would they, themselves, ever consider acting in this way? If so, why? If not, why not?

Students may wish to formulate a series of questions prior to interviewing parents/carers and to use this as the format for these interviews.

Reflection

Ask the students to consider times when they have not felt safe because other people were breaking the rules. For example, when they witness a fight in school or someone refusing to pay their fare on a bus and becoming aggressive or someone trying to steal something from them such as a mobile phone or money. How did they feel? What did they think, say and do? What happened? Would they behave differently next time? If so, how?

Session 12: Coping with Change

Focus

- understanding how change can cause us to feel stressed and anxious

- using coping strategies to cope more effectively with uncomfortable feelings

- knowing that we can choose to have internal control as opposed to being externally controlled

- developing peer support and empathy.

This story is about a boy called Kevin who is just about to transfer to secondary school. He has become increasingly anxious about this move as he feels that he may find it difficult to cope in a bigger school because he is quite a shy and timid person. He is not worried about the work as he feels quite confident in his own abilities. He's mainly worried about meeting and making new friends and being able to find his way around. He has also heard a number of 'horror stories' relating to the school. However, a visit by his new form tutor and some helpful discussions with a good friend help him to feel more positive and to know that he can make good choices in the future.

Either stop the story and discuss the Flag points as you read or read the whole story and use these as discussion points prior to completing the activities.

Green Class had finished their SATs and just returned from school trip. It had been really fantastic and everyone had seemed to have had a great time. Kevin had loved every minute of it. At first, he had been quite nervous about leaving his mum for the whole week. He'd never been away on a holiday unless they had all been together. He wasn't even keen on going to stay at friends' houses. In fact, he'd only every had two sleepovers and these were both at Nick's house. Nick was his cousin and one of the few people that Kevin actually felt truly comfortable with. He was quiet too and they both liked the same kinds of things and didn't get bored as long as there was a computer around or the chance to watch sports on the TV. Neither of them were particularly good at actually doing sports so this seemed like the next best thing. What did amaze

Kevin was the fact that Nick hadn't been able to go on the school journey as he had got a stomach bug at the last minute and yet he had still somehow managed to have good time without his good mate. In fact, what the week had really highlighted was the number of people in his class who were really great – kind, good fun and really able to share good times. Kevin was amazed. He'd joined in with loads of new activities, shared a bunk with Jeffrey Black, sat next to Ellen Chalmers at nearly every meal and learnt at least ten new card games with Ben Tovey. He'd also had a go at bungee jumping and canoeing – two things he thought he'd never do. He'd surprised himself.

Flag: Why do you think some people are shy? What does it actually mean to feel this way? Is it possible to change the way we are or things about our personality? Can we choose to behave differently? What seemed to have helped Kevin during the school trip week?

Anyway, things were now slightly different in that they'd come back to school and there were three weeks left until the end of the term when they had to pretend to do some work. That's what their teacher Mr Jones had said in his usual jokey fashion. However, the reality was that they actually had three weeks to finish off last bits of work, practice their Leaver's Play and prepare to say goodbye to their old school and hello to their new one. Mr Jones was keen that it should be a really nice time for all the students as he wanted them to remember the school in a positive way. He wanted them to have good memories to take with them when they left – that's what he'd said. What it meant was three weeks of very little work and just lots of fun and games and time to be with friends and think about the future.

Flag: How would you like to spend your last three weeks in your current school? What would you like to do? Who would you like to spend time with?

It was all a bit much for Kevin to cope with. It wasn't just the changes he was anticipating at secondary school but also the fact that everything was already so different – too different. It just didn't feel right not to have lessons and it made him nervous not to have the same routine as usual. Also, most of the things they were doing like making photo albums, friendship books and letters and signing each others T-shirts, just seemed to reinforce the fact that things were changing and that they would never be the same again. Kevin didn't want any changes. He'd been OK at Northwood Primary and even now, at this late stage, he'd managed to make friends apart from Nick. How was he going to cope somewhere new? How was he going to get to know people all over again? He wouldn't find it easy. He knew that for a fact. He felt sick and uneasy in his stomach. It was a horrible feeling and he didn't know how he was going to make it go away.

Flag: Change is difficult sometimes and harder for some people than for others. What is making it so difficult for Kevin? What would you advise him to do? What would you do if you were in his position?

The next day he just didn't feel like going to school. He just wanted things to be back to normal and not to change at all. Just as he was leaving the house the phone went. It was Nick. 'How are you?' he asked.

'Alright,' said Kevin lying.

'Look – I know you felt really fed up yesterday, but it will be alright you know. At least we're going to the same school, even if we don't get put in the same form group,' said Nick.

'I know. I just wish I wasn't such a wimp,' sighed Kevin. 'Why couldn't I have been born confident and outgoing like you are? You never seem to be as bad as I am.'

'Hold on, you know I'm not like that. You're just saying that because you feel so bad about yourself at the moment. It's like you saying that everyone else is so much better and stronger and that's just not true. You've got it all wrong just because you're down and stressed. Am I right or am I right?' he said, laughing at himself.

He couldn't ever remember giving a speech like that before but he knew that it was because he genuinely cared about his friend. It was difficult to say it out loud though. No-one talked like that in his family. His dad would call him 'gay' if he ever did.

Flag: Do you think that Nick is a good friend? What is he doing in order to try and support Kevin? What do you think about his dad's opinion? Why is this such an insult? How would you deal effectively with this kind of prejudice?

Nick's mum drove him to school and picked up Kevin on the way. When they got in to the classroom there had been yet another change. The whole room had been changed around so that the chairs were arranged for a Circle Time session.

Kevin said, 'What's going on now? It's not Friday! That's when we normally have Circle Time. Why has it changed?'

They soon found out when Mr Jones came into the room. He wasn't alone. He was accompanied by a short lady with bright red hair, red fingernails and a red dress. She also had the biggest and reddest smile that any of them had ever seen.

'She looks like that film star. You know her,' said Kelly.

'Who? Which one?' asked Ben.

'I don't know her name but she made all the comedies – I wonder if she tells jokes too,' said Kelly. Kevin looked more closely at the new teacher who was introduced to them as Mrs Donaldson. She would be their form tutor in Year 7 and as she started to speak Kevin suddenly and strangely felt himself relax for the first time in what seemed like months. She just sort of had that effect. She wasn't loud or busy. In fact, she wasn't that funny. She was really rather more like Nick than anyone else he'd met before. She talked in a soft, quiet way and you could just tell that she was kind but also someone you wouldn't mess around.

Flag: Do you think you can judge people just on first impressions? Could Kevin have got this wrong? Have you ever made a correct or an incorrect judgement about someone? What happened? Why do people say 'don't judge a book by its cover'? What does this mean?

Anyway, Mrs Donaldson spent the next twenty minutes telling them all about their new High school. She had taken a whole set of photos so that she could show them what each area of the school looked like and all the different places that they would have their lessons. They saw photos of the science labs, the art room, the ICT suite, the drama and sports centres, the swimming pool and the playing fields. She also had a photo of their form room and another of all the members of staff who would be teaching them. She said that she thought it was very important that they could 'put a face to the name'. She pointed out that they would have the core curriculum subjects taught in the same room. So, for the first year, they wouldn't have all the moving around that Kevin had dreaded. The final thing that Mrs Donaldson handed out before they did a Circle Time was an individual 'Welcome Pack' for each member of the class. This really was something special and it was obvious to everyone that a lot of thought and hard work had gone into each document. They included all the information they'd heard in Mrs Donaldson's speech along with copies of the photos and letters from each subject teacher welcoming them to the school and telling them a little bit about themselves and what they might expect from their lessons. Mr Jones said he'd never seen anything like it.

Flag: What do you think of Mrs Donaldson's behaviour? How would it have impacted on the students? What would you like to see in a Welcome Pack? How would you design one?

The Circle Time session was probably even more of a revelation to Kevin. Mrs Donaldson asked all of them to say one thing that they were especially worried about and also to identify one thing that they were really excited about or looking forward to. Everyone had to give their views but you could pass if you really didn't want to say anything. Kevin thought he might just pass. He was feeling slightly more relaxed but he still didn't think he could give his news in front of the others without feeling embarrassed or thinking that they would say he was totally wet. However, it wasn't long before he changed his mind. It seemed that he wasn't the only one who had been feeling stressed about all the changes. He was amazed to hear even the most confident and popular kids saying how they were frightened of meeting older students, worried about making new friends, scared of getting lost, worried about not being able to cope with all the homework and scared that the teachers might be too strict and shout at them if they didn't understand things. There just seemed to be so many worries that all of them shared.

Flag: Why would it be helpful to know that other people felt the same as you? What difference would this make?

Ending point: At this point, the following two endings can be read to the students. The facilitator can then ask the students to judge which is the better ending, that is, which one would achieve the best possible outcome for those involved. The students can then be asked to work out the best ending for themselves via the first Circle Time activity listed in the Activities section.

Ending one

When it came to Kevin's turn he could feel himself going pink in the face. But he somehow knew that he had to take control. He had to stop letting everything seem to get on top of him and control him. He needed to know that he could cope and manage these stresses. After all, he now knew that he'd got friends. He wasn't on his own and he also knew that things weren't going to be quite as scary as he'd first anticipated – not now.

He took a deep breath and said, 'I'm scared of going to secondary school because making friends is hard for me and I think it will be even harder when there's loads of kids and not just a small group like there is here.' He waited. He had expected some laughter but there was just the sort of silence you get when you know others feel exactly the same alongside a few nods in agreement.

Mrs Donaldson smiled and said, 'And what are you excited about? What are you looking forward to Kevin?' He smiled. It was a genuine, big, happy smile. 'Actually,' he said, 'I'm really looking forward to eating in the canteen and having tons to choose from every day – that's one change that will be great.' He stopped for a moment and then said, 'And I think I will be OK – I think I will like it alright because I've chosen to. It's down to me. No-one else.'

Ending two

When it came to Kevin's turn he could feel his stomach churning. He had felt better knowing that others felt like he did. It had also been good to know that the older kids didn't flush your head down the toilet and that you didn't have to have cold showers after PE lessons. But he just couldn't say anything in front of them, certainly not the stuff he was worried about, even if these were similar to their worries. The problem was that they were all far more confident than he was. Even if they were worried, they wouldn't feel as stressed as he did. They'd cope with it better.

That's when he made up his mind – he wouldn't speak out but he would take control, in his own quiet way. He knew he'd be OK but he also knew he'd need some help with this.

'Pass,' he said as Mrs Donaldson looked at him. She smiled and winked at him. He knew it would be alright.

Activities

Use Circle Time as a vehicle to problem-solve. Which ending do the students prefer and why? What kind of help might Kevin and the others need in order to cope with all the changes they were about to encounter? How could they help each other?

Students can consider both the myths and realities of secondary school life. They can draw up a list of all the horror stories they have heard and then formulate a list of associated realities. For example, one myth is that the older students force the Year 7s to stick their heads down the toilets and flush the toilet on top of them. The reality is that this doesn't happen and in many secondary schools the older students often act as mentors for the younger ones, taking them under their wing and helping them to adapt to life in the new school.

Students can design a Welcome Pack for their current school. What would it contain in order to truly welcome a new entrant and enable them to feel included, safe and secure as soon as possible? What would help them cope better with the change process? It may also be helpful for school staff to consider the student's ideas in order to incorporate them into a standardised Welcome Pack for the school.

Work outside school

Students can interview older students who have already successfully made this transition. What helped and hindered them? Who supported them or otherwise? What advice would they give to younger students now? What advice would they give to teachers supporting these students? Students can work together in order to formulate a questionnaire which they feel will give them the most useful information which can, in turn, hopefully inform staff approaches to supporting new students.

Reflection

What small change have you had to cope with? What big change? What were the differences in your feelings, thoughts and behaviours? Did you have any choice about your responses? Would you make different choices as to how to cope and act in the future if similar situations arose?

When you feel worried about tackling something new or different what coping strategies suit you best and why? How can you tell when others aren't coping so well? What can you do and say to help and support them? What would you like to change about yourself now and why? Can you set yourself some goals? What are you aiming for? What are your wishes and dreams and how can you make good choices in order to make them a reality?